State Capitalism Reforms and the Path for Belarus

Praise for the Book

"This book is a coffee table handbook for anyone interested in the Belarusian economy".
—Mikhail Golosov
Professor of Economics, Princeton University, USA

"In a pragmatic, reasoned study, the author outlines the current structure of the Belarusian economy and explains how it came to be; but more importantly he lays out a course for continued reforms and argues how the best to take the country's brand of 'state capitalism' into a stable, prosperous future".
—Courtney Fingar
Editor-in-chief, fDi Magazine (FT Group), UK

"In addition to being profound, multi-faceted and critical in its analysis, this book is very timely – the Belarusian economy is on the threshold of inevitable structural changes – and it is a practical guide for introducing such changes to the public finances".
—Dmytro Sologub
Deputy Governor, National Bank of Ukraine

"This book is food for thought when it comes to Belarus' future economic model. A profound understanding of the economic state Belarus finds itself in, and the factors used to build the paradigm for the country's development over the course of the past several years, needs to drive new, workable solutions that resolve economic imbalances, bolster growth and large-scale energy consumption, and feed the dynamism intrinsic to the private sector".
—Dimitri Gvindadze
Lead Economist for East Europe and the Caucasus of the European Bank for Reconstruction and Development; ex-Minister of Finance of Georgia

State Capitalism Reforms and the Path for Belarus:

Financial Diet

By

Kiryl Rudy

Cambridge Scholars Publishing

State Capitalism Reforms and the Path for Belarus: Financial Diet

By Kiryl Rudy

This book first published 2020

Cambridge Scholars Publishing

Lady Stephenson Library, Newcastle upon Tyne, NE6 2PA, UK

British Library Cataloguing in Publication Data
A catalogue record for this book is available from the British Library

ISBN (10): 1-5275-5859-2
ISBN (13): 978-1-5275-5859-5

To my wife Elena,
and my sons Anton and Ilya

CONTENTS

INTRODUCTION

The region Belarus calls home has been wracked by turbulence. The tectonic shifts of the 1980s led to new countries arising from the rubble of the Soviet empire in a way that has been entirely new. Nowadays, the post-Soviet space is revisiting key issues like strategic choice, peace, and territorial integrity. Many countries, having never built an economic normalcy, find themselves in a new reality that casts a long shadow over their future.

Belarus is more than capable of a surprise or two. In the 1990s, this medium-sized European country took its first steps on its own, and it has spent the intervening decades sticking closely to the choices it made then. However, and for the first time since then, in 2015, and until now, its economy skidded to a near-complete halt. What happens next? Will it lean on its obscurity and unpredictability to surprise once more, or will it test the depths of its resolve by staying the course? Unfortunately, that question is, as of yet, unanswerable. The myriad rational, irrational, internal, and external factors that come into play simply cannot all be accounted for, or even foreseen, not to mention the fact that economics are not the determinant when it comes to the solution. Time, then, is the only judge, and time alone will show which path should have been taken.

The outlook for the Belarusian economy is bleak. The post-Soviet economic structure and manual management is at the end of its rope. Budget spending, devaluations, and debt, no longer help fuel economic growth, and relatively free and long-term access to money has distorted economic stimuli. The system of incentives in place for state-owned enterprises is holding back initiative and innovation, and the continuous flow of state capital conceals mistakes in management. But the problem runs deeper: the consistently preferential treatment enjoyed by the public sector drives costs higher and keeps market resources out of the hands of the private sector, strangling its development as well. All of that saps energy and enthusiasm in the country, and puts a damper on growth. And economic growth must be in place in order to enjoy social stability.

The need for reforms might seem to be self-evident. Like oars on a boat sailing upstream, without them the economy is carried backwards by the current. Private initiative also plays a role, serving as a following wind.

Unfortunately, those reforms are being held back by a lack of direction. Manual management[1] of the economy is so overwhelming that it leaves neither strength nor time for strategic decisions, and with the new generation has come a shift away from nostalgia—a tendency to look for the future in the past—towards uncertainty. No attention is paid to setting clear priorities for a new Belarusian economy. This keeps complex decisions from being made, and serves to oversimplify the situation. The lack of reforms is also explained by an unwillingness to take responsibility for the social fallout. That psychological barrier can only be overcome by recognizing the inevitability of transformation; it is self-awakening that will illuminate the path forward for reforms.

The Belarusian economy is naturally evolving. The private sector is developing, and small business is growing, as well as the service industry. On the other hand, the efforts being made to preserve old state-owned manufacturing and the mobilization model, are limiting the economy's flexibility.

The financial diet referred to in the title of this book is a framework for reforming the economy. It is not shock therapy. It does include well-ordered, rational redistribution of state financial resources. In finance, just as in medicine, a 'diet' (from the Greek word for 'lifestyle') tries to structure an organism as best it can, making it more flexible and stable. For people, that means creating healthy stimuli towards an active way of life, vitality, and consumption in moderation. A financial diet reminds us that capital is a resource, and is just as non-renewable as oil, gas, or even time.

This book is for those who want to dig into how the Belarusian economy works. Its readers want to understand what Belarusians call normal, and how often, and to what degree, that wish is rational. This financial diet is a choice, not only between consuming and saving, or between 'want' and 'need' but, fundamentally, between rational and normal 'ingredients'.

The main driver for the economic recession in Belarus is its lack of capital, without which state capitalism cannot function. That mortal threat to the state, therefore, has to be de-fanged by private or foreign capital before the economy can return to growth. Ultimately, the path out of economic stagnation, called here 'a *financial diet*', is increasing capital efficiency.

The book consists of three parts:

Part 1 reveals the case of Belarus – the country 'trapped in transition'. After the break up of the Soviet Union, Belarus failed to implement classical market reforms: there was no privatization of large state-owned enterprises, no 'shock therapy' in price liberalization, no free movement of labour and capital. Gradual, step-by-step economic policy created a hybrid economic regime with the collabouration of private and state sectors, export-oriented IT in services, and collective farms in agriculture, 'manual management' in the machinery-building industry, and corporate management in the banking field, high level redistribution of financial flows through the budget, and active roles played by state-owned banks and the sovereign fund. All these characterize the Belarusian model of state capitalism.

Due to the pitfalls facing Belarus' economy, Belarusian state capitalism is trapped in transition. The external and internal financing deficits have led to long-term economic stagnation. Lack of innovation, social overfinancing, the 'resource curse', and situations with conflicting neighbors, lock the country into the 'middle-income trap'. Such a stable economic anemia brings the country either to the eve of social instability, or to the unavoidance of economic reforms.

Part 2 shows plenty of 'transformer' countries; successful stories of transition. A group of 26 economies from Central and Eastern Europe and CIS went through two periods of transition: adaptation to new economic environments and development. Why was the first group more successful than the second one on that road? It's because Central and Eastern European countries were motivated to become EU members, which kept them on track and pushed the reforms. That political will helped them to overcome the 'middle-income trap', while Russia, as an example of a country without such external leverage left the 'middle-income' trap and then fell back into it.

China is another success story of unstoppable reforms rewarded by sustainable high economic growth. The country went through different models of transformation: from an administrative to a market economy, from being export-oriented to consumption-driven, from industry towards a service sector. As the result of faster reforms, in 2015, China overtook Belarus in GDP per capita, in 2019 it overtook Kazakhstan, and in 2020, it overtook Russia.

Part 3 provides the manual for economic reforms in transition economies. It starts with answers to the simple questions: 'why', 'where to', 'how', 'what', 'who', 'for whom', etc. The decision makers, reformers, and economic authorities should follow the logic of priorities, strategy, structure, and personnel. That will reveal the mechanisms for economic reforms.

The path out of the 'transition trap' for Belarus starts with the financial diet. Macroeconomic stability, long-term financial equilibrium, and the raising of public funds efficiently will create the need for finalizing economic transition: privatization, price liberalization, and free movement of labour and capital. Without these reforms, the financial diet will bring the country to a state of financial hunger, economic recession, and finally into social turmoil. So, the financial diet is only the first step on the way out of the transition trap. As always, it's the most difficult step, but it is also the most important.

Part 1.

"Trapped in Transition": The Case of Belarus

CHAPTER 1

STATE CAPITALISM IN BELARUS

The Republic of Belarus features an unstable market economy in the early stages of its development. A variety of economic relationships which are constantly in flux are coupled with complexity and unpredictability; market elements jostle with state planning and manual management. On the one hand, the country features state ownership of large swathes of property, administrative (manual) control over state-owned enterprises, directed lending, consolidated budgetary resources, and far-reaching social security. On the other hand, it has its entrepreneurs, small and medium-sized businesses, private and foreign businesses, a liberal banking sector, a free-floating exchange rate, market pricing, elements of a public-private partnership, a functioning Hi-Tech Park, China-Belarus Industrial Park "Great Stone", free economic zones, and other aspects of a market economy.

The special nature of the Belarusian economy is sometimes reminiscent of other countries: modern Russia in the face of sanctions, other post-Soviet countries, and also China, at one point in its development. The resemblance is especially clear when talking about the active role played by the government in a market economy, something generally referred to as state capitalism. State capitalism is understood here to be an economy in which the state plays the main role as entrepreneur, employer, owner of the means of production, and profit allocator.

With that said, there are a few important things to note when considering Belarus' particular brand of state capitalism:

1. The reasons for its birth and longevity;
2. Its current state, as compared to other countries across a number of metrics;
3. The tools used to make it function.

The origins of state capitalism in Belarus

1) The legacy of the Soviet Union

1.1) Administrative management experience

The Soviet planned economy (and its management) was tangled, cumbersome, and excessively theoretical. The Central Committee established an ideological direction for economic policy, while the government (Council of Ministers) performed what was often a highly technical function. Of course, Gosplan was at the heart of the Soviet economy. It distributed funds and resources for which regions, ministries, and enterprises, competed. That access to financial resources created the context for manual control, or for managing projects by manually distributing money. Inter-departmental haggling for financial resources resulted in plans, limits, and other services which sometimes suffered from a lack of transparency.[2] In practice, the Soviet economy was run, and functioned, thanks to a multitude of ambiguous interpretations and loopholes. Even when there were shortages of certain goods, they could still be found, as long as one knew how to work the system. Official policy created room for a shadow equivalent, and decisions were sometimes interpreted in completely opposite ways, depending on the circumstances. Other decisions were ignored altogether. That experience was common to all the former Soviet republics.

The fall of the Soviet Union gave birth to an 'anti-crisis management model'[3] in Belarus which included a strong administration, manual management at all levels, and multiple controls. That post-Soviet model followed in the footsteps of Soviet administrative management, secrecy, centralized control, and the Soviet view of the institution of power through the prism of control over property, the budget, and labour resources. However, manual management is only possible when there are financial resources available to distribute between projects. Financial deficits reduce management to handing out instructions which are no longer backed by real money, leading to increased debt, liquidity problems for businesses and banks, and distorted funding for other public sectors. Ultimately, those financial and monetary distortions spread, to infect the economy as a whole, as well as influencing the behavior of economic entities.

Soviet approaches to management were also propped up by the sanctions imposed on Belarus by the US and the EU. That partly explains the orientation of the country's management style towards the USSR in many respects, in some respects towards Russia, and in yet others, towards China. The biggest foreign investors and lenders in Belarus, for example, have been Russian companies and banks, while the China-Belarus Industrial Park "Great Stone" near Minsk serves as more proof of the country's long-standing leaning towards the East.

1.2) Soviet economic structure

State capitalism in Belarus was built on the legacy of the Soviet economic structure, featuring large industrial and agricultural sectors. From 1922 to 1991, Belarus created, on average, 4.2% of the Soviet Union's GDP, manufactured 11.3% of its refrigerators, and 10.8% of its televisions, and produced 7% of its milk. It also featured a traditionally open economy: it was the second Soviet republic after Russia in terms of exports outside the countries belonging to the Council for Mutual Economic Assistance. In 1990, manufacturing made up 70% of Belarus' GDP. Many manufacturing giants from the Soviet years, for example, the Minsk Automobile Plant, the Minsk Tractor Works, and BelAZ, were held onto by the state, and slowly evolved into symbols of the modern Belarusian economy. Corporate connections dating back to the Soviet Union, and state support, have helped industrial state-owned enterprises to maintain the market positions they have traditionally held.

The notorious experience of privatization in Russia and the Ukraine in the 1990s had a restraining effect on the privatization of industrial enterprises in Belarus. Public disapproval of the large-scale privatization in Russia still echoes in the ears of Belarusian decision-makers. Not only that, but the state support that Belarusian state-owned companies received impacted the prices at which they could be sold, and the disparity between government investment and the real value of sales held back, or even prevented, their privatization. Of course, given the country's underdeveloped institutions and markets, it is important to note that a complete sell-off of such companies by the government could sabotage the trust placed in them from abroad, their credit ratings, the investment they attract, and their profitability. That problem is avoidable, as long as the international rating of the new investors and owners is higher than that of Belarus.

1.3) Socialism

The mobilization management model in Belarus drove social stability and enjoyed public popularity in the 1990s, especially when contrasted with the social turbulence experienced in neighboring countries. Belarusian society also held a degree of nostalgia for the relatively successful social and economic development that Belarus had grown accustomed to as part of the Soviet Union. As a result, Belarusian state capitalism had the support and understanding of the people as a form of socialism, or a welfare state.

Society's expectation that a social government should see and account for everything is clearly unrealistic. Just as Gosplan (during the time of the Soviet Union) was unable to collect all the information it needed and take into account all the needs of the population, leading to shortages, socialism that includes the participation of the government as a market entity cannot resist the temptation to set up monopolies and regulate prices. In addition, the post-Soviet variety of socialism overinflates social expectations, preserving cross-subsidization, equity construction, and other distorted business models. Excessive socialization also cuts the legs out from under private initiative, something that can only be compensated for by a public-private partnership as part of the government's social function.

2) Internal reasons for state capitalism in Belarus

2.1) Underdeveloped institutions

Setting up a market economy involves creating institutions to protect property rights, the rule of law, competitive business practices, transparency and accountability in government, effective state management, et al. While that is generally a long and difficult process, in Belarus' nascent market economy, it was compensated for by a state capitalism that saw the institutional role of the government grow in tandem. For example, in 2020 Belarus held the following positions in international institutional ratings:

A) 49th out of 189 countries in a ranking by the World Bank for ease of doing business that looks at the expenses borne by companies who interact with government institutions as well as infrastructure development;

B) 66th out of 180 countries in a ranking of international transparency that compares levels of corruption.

As a rule, underdeveloped formal economic institutions leave a vacuum filled by inside sources, corruption, confidential relationships, and informal agreements. That trust-based model of informal rules has come to be called 'social capital' in literature, and it includes one's personal network, reputation, ethical norms, and moral values.[4] It is important to note the fact that that a model of informal institutions is built from the bottom up, and accounts for national quirks and traditions. On the whole it is entirely capable of functioning and even successful: it often guarantees property and capital rights in addition to stimulating economic growth. For example, social capital is pointed to as the reason for northern Italy's climb past its southern cousin. With that said, informal rules on their own serve the interests of the strong. It is only when they also serve the interests of others that they can be useful to society and morph into formal rules. The need to protect public interests is what makes state institutions essential, given that private interests are generally determined by the market.

There are a number of ways governments can combat informal institutions by imposing their formal counterparts from the top down. For example, Singapore uses the British legal system to smooth away distrust for national legislation, while China still struggles with corruption. Belarus leverages myriad agreements in conjunction with cross control and a complaints policy. While the Belarusian model has its advantages, its weakness is that each state entity has the ability to hit the brakes on decision-making by looking back, and leaning on controlling authorities and possibly private complaints. That leads to foot-dragging, and sometimes it is impossible to get anything done. Final business solutions are often put off and become unpredictable: the early 1990s saw some local businessmen export capital and bring it back into the country via foreign investors. Investors try to build relationships and even joint ventures with the authorities and security services in an attempt to hang onto their capital. Ultimately, property rights are only as secure as the status and career of their holder.

Developing economic institutions is a long process that needs a mature society. Transitioning to an institutionalized economy for developing countries means concluding the initial buildup of capital as well as moving away from state and private monopolies. That means that the government willingly imposes competition, often to the detriment of existing players. As this process progresses, big business is most concerned with protecting property rights, while small business is preoccupied by administrative barriers keeping them from entering the market in addition to securing a guarantee of fair competition. It is also important to maintain currently existing property rights when moving to an institutionalized economy. Public support for distributing property rights only happens if there is a large number of shareholders in the country with respect for those rights. Arguably no less important is economic amnesty that lets market players legalize under-the-table earnings from previous eras and start fresh with a clean slate. Not only is the role of undergirding formal institutions (itself, at the end of the day) played by the government important when it comes to institutional change; society plays a key role by acting as a counterpart to the government.

2.2) Public support

State capitalism in Belarus enjoys public support thanks to income growth and moderate inequality:

A) While the average monthly salary in the 1990s came to a few tens of dollars,[5] by 2006 it had grown to 271, and in 2014 it reached a 25-year high of 595 dollars. In early 2016 it dropped to 300 dollars, and in May 2020 it was 476 dollars. Purchasing power also grew over the same period. For example, from 2010 to 2014, the purchasing power of an average month's salary when it comes to foodstuffs (chicken, oil, fish, potatoes, sausage) rose by 20–70%, also growing 70–90% for consumer durables (refrigerators, washing machines, cars).

B) In 1990 the inequality index (GINI index from 0 to 1, with 1 signifying extreme inequality) in Belarus was 0.24, in 2000 it was 0.23, in 2010 it was 0.27, in 2013 it was 0.26, and in 2018 it was 0.25. That number looks even better when juxtaposed with those of other countries featuring high levels of state involvement in the economy. For example, in Russia in 1991 it was 0.26 before rising to 0.44 in 2018; in China it was 0.33 in 1990 and 0.47 in 2018. It's interesting to mention here, that in the book about the history of inequality *The Great Leveler* by Walter Scheidel, the author positioned the inequality as a normal state of capitalism and human nature. Analyzing the cases from the Stone Age to the 21st century, he concludes that the great levelers were wars, revolutions, state collapses, plagues, and violence in general.[6]

It is most likely that those two factors suppress the need for a move away from state capitalism in Belarus and towards faster-paced development of institutions. After all, the push for institutional change most often comes from the middle class, and sometimes from the political elite.

Literature delineates four ways to transform economic models while also building and developing institutions influenced by changing levels and paces of income growth and inequality:[7]

1) A long, gradual move toward stable democratic institutions stimulated by long-term economic growth (see Great Britain);
2) Speedy creation of democratic institutions and their equally speedy collapse into high income inequality, social discontent, and a faltering economic (see Argentina);
3) A lack of democracy coupled with high or growing income levels that suits the population (see Singapore);
4) A dictatorship with high income inequality, exploitation, and forcible pressure that slows the economy (see South Africa).

Those options give way to each other under the influence of economic and political crises. Dictatorships crumble under the weight of social protests, while democracies are overthrown by populism or military coups.[8] Hybrid options are also feasible: for instance, so-called competitive authoritarianism, a category to which literature assigns post-Soviet political and economic models.[9]

Obviously, the best option is the evolutionary formation of institutions exemplified by Great Britain. At the same time, that is only possible once a set income level is reached and a strong middle class has been established, preventing constant waffling between models and creating a stable social push and long-term support for institutional change and continued institutional growth. The middle class, though, does not appear in a country naturally; instead, it is carefully nurtured by state policy. For example, in China, the average monthly income over the period from 2013 to 2015 has been 500-700 dollars, later from 2016 to 2019 – 800-900 dollars while the cap of income not subject to income tax was set at a bit lower than 500 dollars per month and then increased in 2019 to 735 dollars. That drives the appearance of a middle class brandishing new demands for institutional change in both the economic and political arenas.

We cannot but note that educating society by influencing public opinion is a critical issue when it comes to developing institutions in a country and attaining public support for reform. That is the role played by economists who have to regularly explain current policy, possible alternatives for society, or even the lack of an economic policy. For example, Ludwig Erhard in Germany gave a weekly address over the radio that dealt with economic issues. He also required his subordinates to talk to people when visiting on business, filling them in on what was going on. Ignoring the gravity of problems robs their solutions of urgency and weakens public support for reform.

State capitalism in Belarus is an evolved, post-Soviet model for economic development and socialism that enjoys popularity and public support. It has its own features setting it apart as well as similarities to other countries, something borne out by a number of metrics.

State capitalism metrics in Belarus

The similarities and differences between Belarusian state capitalism and its foreign counterparts can be measured by looking at how the state intervenes in the economy: public expenditures to GDP, the tax burden, and the role of state-owned enterprises in the economy (portion of GDP created, jobs created, etc.).

1) Public expenditures to GDP

This indicator shows how consolidated budgetary funds are in an economy. In Belarus in 2010 – 2019 they were, on average, around 30% of GDP, though adding in social security pushes that number to an internationally recognized *40% of GDP*. At the same time, middle-income countries are said to be unable to sustain economic growth if they redistribute more than 30% of GDP via a consolidated budget.[10] By way of comparison: CIS countries registered at 27%; Central and Eastern Europe at 34%; and Brazil, India, Korea, Malaysia, Singapore, and South Africa at an average of 22%.

This number is higher for developed countries than it is for developing ones. For instance, for G7 countries it was at an average of 31%. A number of countries (the US and France in particular) sometimes boost public spending as an anticyclical tool used to stimulate growth and maintain strong social welfare. However, that most likely only works for countries issuing a reserve currency, boasting a developed financial market, and capable of converting inflationary pressure into savings and investment. For Belarus, boosting public spending could serve to slow economic growth in addition to triggering inflation. Increased public spending stimulates consumer and manufacturing imports, negatively impacting GDP.

It is difficult to pin down the connection between this metric and an economy's level of development. Correlation analysis of state spending to GDP and per capita GDP in terms of purchasing power parity over the period from 2000 to 2012 came up with correlation coefficients that were far from 1. For CIS countries it was 0.04, for Central and Eastern

European countries it was 0.37, for developing countries it was -0.68, for G7 countries it was -0.41, and for Belarus it was 0.19.

2) Tax burden

Belarus enjoys a lighter tax burden than many developed countries. In 2019 tax revenue, including social spending, came to 37% of GDP. Tax burden, without social spending, was 25% in 2019 and has stayed flat since 2016.[11]

Developed countries saw that same number range from 33% to 55% between 2000 and 2019. Interestingly, from 1870 to 1910 in developed countries it was as low as 7–8%, and was sufficient for governments to pay for security, legal systems, foreign services, and everything else the public needed.[12] The growth in tax revenue experienced by those countries since then has primarily served to cover spending on social programs and infrastructure. For the same reason, Belarus has a fairly high tax burden, with around 12% of GDP going to social security.

3) The role of state-owned enterprises in the economy

Opinions differ when it comes to evaluating the role of state-owned enterprises in the Belarusian economy. According to the National Statistical Committee of the Republic of Belarus (Belstat), in 2019 state-owned companies created around half of GDP in Belarus. While comparable to Russia's 50%, in China, for example, state-owned companies take up only around 30% of GDP,[13] and the total around the world is only 6% of global GDP.

Another way of looking at this issue is to evaluate the contribution state-owned enterprise in Belarus makes to the budget, its foreign exchange earnings (about 30% in 2019), the jobs it creates (43%), industry production (73.3%), retail turnover (16.2%), and revenue (58%).[14] On the other hand, the close relationship between public and private business in Belarus makes it difficult to objectively determine the role played by the public side of that partnership independent of its private counterpart.

One distinctive feature of public enterprise in Belarus is its scale: state-owned enterprises support an entire ecosystem comprised of hundreds of smaller state-owned, private, and foreign suppliers, contractors, and intermediaries. In keeping with international terminology, companies critical to the economy vis-à-vis manufacturing, taxes, exports, and employment, are designated 'national champions'. However, the fact that they are occasionally forced to lay off employees, reduce production, and rely on tax breaks to maintain competitiveness means that the list of Belarusian national champions sometimes changes. Interestingly, that list periodically includes service-oriented companies as well as both private and foreign-owned companies thanks to the Wimbledon effect, which is when national tournaments are won by foreigners (see Table 1).

Table 1: National champions in Belarus, 2014[15]

Category	Company name	Ownership
Largest manufacturers (by volume in terms of actual selling prices)	Belaruskali	State-owned
	Belarusian Steel Works	State-owned
	Minsk Automobile Plant	State-owned
	Minsk Tractor Works	State-owned
	Minskenergo	State-owned
Largest taxpayers (by share of budget revenue)	Gazprom Transgaz Belarus (4.9%)	Foreign
	Belaruskali (3.8%)	State-owned
	Naftan (3.5%)	State-owned
	Mozyr Oil Refinery (3.5%)	Join (state-owned, foreign)
	Lukoil Belarussia (2.5%)	Foreign
	Grodno Tobacco Factory "Neman" (2.3%)	State-owned
	Tabak-Invest (1%)	Private
	Minsk Grape Wines Factory (1%)	Private
Largest exporters	Belarusian Oil Company	State-owned
	RN-West	Private
	Belarusneft	State-owned
	Belarusian Steel Works	State-owned
	InterService	Private
Largest employers (by number of employees)	Evrotorg (22,600)	Private
	Belpochta (20,500)	State-owned
	Belarusbank (19,500)	State-owned
	Minsk Automobile Plant (18,800)	State-owned
	Minsk Tractor Works (18,800)	State-owned
	Beltelecom (17,800)	State-owned
	Belaruskali (17,600)	State-owned

4) Share of employment at state-owned enterprises

This indicator deserves a separate look due to its economic and social importance for Belarus. State-owned enterprises made up 43.4% of employment in Belarus as of January 1, 2020,[16] 39% of employment in Russia, 19% of employment in China, and 3% of employment in France.

The high percentage of employment generated by state-owned enterprises in Belarus is in large measure due to how connected they are to individual cities, something left over from the Soviet Union. From a social point of view, that makes them essential; from an economic point of view it keeps labour resources sticky and puts a damper on overall labour productivity across wide swaths of territory. However, there are a number of historical examples that point to a way out of that conundrum by reorienting both the companies and the cities with which they are so intrinsically connected. For example, factories in the Ruhr (Germany) were transformed into centers of creative industry, while an entertainment industry and eco-tech cluster were also founded. In Birmingham (USA) the coal and steel industries gave way to a healthcare center that includes medical services, education, and research. Manchester (UK) went from a textiles city to a cultural capital, attracting world-class musicians, investors, and tourists.[17] A similar transformation happened in Beijing (China), when an old East German factory was transformed into the popular Art Zone '798'.

High employment at state owned enterprises in Belarus can be seen as providing social security in the form of guaranteed jobs (lifetime employment). However, companies incapable of holding up on their own under intense competition cannot provide that security to their employees. Counting on the government to continually prop them up can distort public finances and lead to problems for other public services, also preventing manpower from migrating to industries characterized by higher added value and stronger economic growth.[18] Social support is better served by creating new jobs, and thereby offering a choice as opposed to guaranteeing employment. The government can leverage market-based methods to avoid hidden unemployment and the costs involved in maintaining employment, keeping social policy from undermining economic policy.[19]

Looking at the metrics measuring state capitalism in Belarus helps compare it to other countries at the macro level with regard to public spending and the tax burden. Belarusian quirks appear more at the micro level in the role state-owned enterprise plays in the economy, particularly by providing employment. Private and foreign-owned companies also play a visible role in the Belarusian economy.

Tools for state capitalism in Belarus

1) State-owned (and private) enterprises

State-owned enterprises are the main tool Belarus has for state capitalism. It is believed that the economy could be run as if it were a single state-owned corporation, and thus managed more efficiently. The government participates in the day-to-day management of individual companies by setting goals, approving business plans, helping organize sales, unloading warehouses, continually monitoring operations, attracting financing for agriculture, and running social projects, sports, and more. By way of comparison, the Chinese government limits itself to managing its state-owned enterprises at the strategic level. Directors sign three-year contracts and are given long-term goals. Russia, in turn, mixes strategic and operational management: state agencies establish long-term plans and goals, though they have been getting more involved with purchasing, contractor selection, and pricing.

1.1) Direct planning

In 2014 a plan was laid out for state-owned enterprises: Order 585 of the President of Belarus to the government dated December 31 2013, set out nine parameters outlining the plan for the country's social and economic development in 2014.

1) GDP
2) Labour productivity
3) Exports of goods and services
4) Balance of trade in goods and services
5) Foreign direct investment
6) Energy consumption
7) Private income
8) New housing construction
9) Inflation

That order included Resolution 17 by the Council of Ministers dated January 13 2014, which included seven metrics for state-owned enterprises:

1) Growth rate for exports of goods
2) Growth rate for exports of services
3) Ratio of goods exports to production
4) Revenue per worker
5) Growth in revenue per worker in excess of growth in nominal wages
6) Sales profitability
7) Energy savings

Local authorities add their own metrics to that list, including physical production volumes, because standards for gross regional product are set for Minsk and the country's regions. Local authorities, therefore, set goals for the enterprises located in their area of responsibility, sometimes for both state- and privately owned firms.

It is important to note that the number of state enterprises subject to centrally determined metrics is dropping. While in the 1990s it included almost all of them, in 2010 it dropped to 140 before falling still further, to around 80, in 2019. Most recently it is primarily the manufacturing industry, responsible for a bit more than 20% of GDP, that receives directed plans from the government. As for non-state-owned companies, administrative pressure is occasionally exerted on them to conform to state-set goals by signing special contracts or 'gentlemen's agreements'.

1.2) Anti-crisis management of public enterprise

State and local authorities often serve as anti-crisis managers, actively intervening and periodically offering support to state-owned enterprises. For example, in 2015, the government and the National Bank took control of the business plans for 106 of them with the heaviest external debt burdens.

Anti-crisis management encompasses the use of a number of financial tools: tax breaks, short-term loans, debt restructuring, loan servicing, and more. The problem is that a conflict of interests necessarily arises between the Ministry of Finance and the government agency responsible for a particular state enterprise (the ministry for that industry or the local authority, for example). Sometimes, and for a number of state-owned enterprises, temporary state support turns out to be permanent, at which point their incentive is to work for that support as opposed to meeting customer needs. In those situations, as well as those in which there is a monopoly (state-owned or private), there is no need to fight off competitors, haggle with buyers, or please clients. That relaxes business, stifling initiative and innovation. However, once administrative resources begin to run out, or new officials and priorities are brought in, state support begins to wane, exposing inherent weaknesses.

Manual anti-crisis management and long-term state support propping up industrial enterprises engender familiarity among many, as well as a suspicion of other forms of management. An anti-crisis posture and way of thinking becomes the norm. Some oppose private and foreign business to the point of rejecting privatizations, while others jump into the opposite ditch of seeing absolute privatization as a silver bullet. An equally polarized attitude is taken to state-owned companies themselves: the first group sees them as holding the economy back, while the second thinks of them as engines suffering from a temporary setback.

1.3) Administrative burden

State and local authorities often hold meetings, summits, and panel discussions that include both state-owned and sometimes private firms, send instructions, request statistics, and recommend sponsorships. A survey of 800 directors of Belarusian firms, run in 2013 by the Economy Research Institute of the Ministry of Economy, found that 71% of those surveyed spend at least 20% of each week (one working day) on meetings with state agencies, the main topic of which, 91% say, is meeting set metrics. With that in mind, private firms increasingly prefer to avoid contact with the government in an effort to avoid that administrative pressure.

However, what is felt more keenly are the inspections the state has been running recently as part of its goal to limit imports. According to the Association of Retail Networks, there has been an uptick in the number of inspections conducted by the Ministry of Trade since December 2014. Traded goods themselves are also subject to inspection by the State Control Committee, several departments in the Ministry of Internal Affairs, the Ministry for Emergency Situations, the Ministry for Taxes and Levies, the Ministry of Labour and Social Protection, the Ministry of Natural Resources and Environmental Protection, the State Committee for Standardization, local authorities, and other monitoring and law enforcement agencies. Although the process is legally regulated, the administrative burden pushes operational costs higher for businesses.

In general, top-down regulation under Belarus' state capitalism breeds conformism, bureaucratic red tape, and corruption. The usual powerful idea as to why the country should limit the share of state-owned enterprises in the economy is that people don't fully take care of things that don't belong to them. In Belarus they treat state-owned enterprises as though they are collectively owned, the people's,or national, mostly a matter of pride, rather than profit. In the discussion of state vs. private enterprise, the case of Belarus shows that all of the state enterprises can expect budget subsidies and government bail-outs. On the other hand it cannot be guaranteed that corruption issues will be solved after enterprises are privatized. Moreover, Belarusian statistics show that private companies are charged with fines by tax authorities more than state-owned companies, (this could be also be explained by the attitude of the government towards the private sector).

2) Banks

Banks are a significant tool used to finance state capitalism in Belarus. They can be divided into state banks, banks with foreign capital, and the Development Bank, and each category has its own set purpose. However, the banking system in Belarus does not satisfy the country's economic needs, meaning that it suffers from chronic undercapitalization. The Belarusian banking system commanded assets equalling a bit more than 60% of GDP in 2013, and 57% in 2019. In Russia, that number is 86%; in Ukraine it is 91%; in Hungary, Poland, and the Czech Republic it is 100 – 110%; in China and Japan it is around 150%; and in France and the UK it exceeds 200%.

2.1) State-owned banks

The lion's share of the Belarusian banking system is occupied by two state-owned banks: Belarusbank and Belagroprombank. They participate in state programs and offer state support, commanding a monopoly of the banking system vis-à-vis assets (62.2% between them as of April 1 2020) and capital (60.4%).[20] The low profitability that comes with state programs and support, ranks state-owned banks among the country's worst large banks in terms of asset profitability and capital.

Administrative meddling in the day-to-day operations of state banks by oversight boards often leads to directed lending that does not take the bank's reserves into consideration, creating liquidity issues. Directed lending also relieves banks of responsibility for channeling funds towards underperforming projects. When the general economic situation worsens or revenue dries up, companies no longer have the ability to service the loans held by banks. Moreover, the high cost of rouble-denominated loans pushed many state-owned enterprises in 2013–2014 to move over to cheaper loans denominated in foreign currencies. Changing exchange rates added weight to their debt load and future devaluations could make it tough to service bank loans. The continually changing outlook also ensures a constant stream of bank customers switching their accounts to and from roubles, as well as into and out of the banking system, draining bank reserves. All those factors intensify the systemic risks faced by banks, and a state infusion of capital, or moving toxic assets to the Development Bank or public debt when directed lending is relaxed, serves as only a temporary reprieve for the banking system.

Another problem is that Belarusbank and Belagroprombank, though they have the same owner, do not always coordinate their efforts to perform their social function and end up echoing each other. For example, their locations and banking service centers are located on the same street in almost every town across the country (often even where there are few people living). Sberbank of Russia, by comparison, successfully streamlines its branch network, while in Switzerland, Italy, and France banking functions are handled by post offices in remote areas.

When it comes to the issue of making Belarusian state-owned banks more efficient, China's experience boosting capital for its state banks by attracting foreign direct investment while still regaining control is intriguing. For each major state-owned bank the government found a strategic minority investor (Bank of America, Goldman Sachs), adopted management and banking technology, and then capitalized them via an initial public offering. The IPO of Chinese state-owned banks was the largest in the world. In one example the Agricultural Bank of China brought in more than 19 billion dollars from the market in a single day (July 6 2010).

2.2) Banks with foreign capital

The share of foreign banks in the Belarusian banking system is not as large: on April 1 2020, it was 34.7% of assets and 35.2% of capital.[21] Even so, banks with foreign (primarily Russian) capital do impact the development of the Belarusian economy. Access to relatively cheap resources from their parent banks as well as professional management and technology lets them offer loans to Belarusian companies with better conditions and service than their state-owned counterparts. As a result, foreign banks work with more active, profitable, and up-and-coming Belarusian firms. For example, in 2014, companies like Belarusneft and Tabak-Invest were financed completely by banks with foreign credit, the Mozyr Oil Refinery obtained 97% of its financing through foreign banks,

Naftan 78%, the Minsk Automobile Plant, and Amkodor around 60%, and Grodno Azot and the Grodno Tobacco Factory 'Neman' 55%. There were several attempts to move the accounts of state-owned enterprises from foreign banks to state-owned banks. But it was hard to implement.

Half of all foreign loans extended to the Belarusian banking system, in 2014 and later, were from Russia. Unfortunately, Russian loans have been getting more expensive recently, due to the capital outflow from Russia, sanctions, and the Russian economic slowdown. The global era of cheap money may also be ending: the US Federal Reserve plans to boost the interest rate at some point in the coming years. The Belarusian economy needs financing for banks with foreign capital to remain open and maintain current interest rates, something that can sometimes be achieved by administrative and political means.

2.3) Development Bank of the Republic of Belarus

In 2011, the Development Bank was founded as a non-banking institution designed to improve the economic performance of government investment programs. From December 2011 to June 2013, Belarusbank and Belagroprombank handed over some of their state program assets to the newly founded institution, altogether totalling more than 12 trillion roubles. They did hold onto some old loans and continue lending directly to government programs.

As of 2019, an old mechanism for funding state programs in Belarus was still in place, though it keeps the Development Bank from being able to perform its primary function. If that mechanism changes, or a competitive, results-based approach is taken to distributing funds, the Development Bank can transition to the traditional format employed by development banks in other countries (for example, in Germany, China, and Russia). The Belarusian Development Bank could then focus on providing export finance, financing major infrastructure projects, supporting small and medium business, and on the country's other priority goals.

3) National Development Fund

Sovereign development funds are a tool used by many governments to redistribute financial resources around the economy. There are currently 60 of them, with the largest being in the United Arab Emirates,

Norway, Saudi Arabia, China, Singapore, Russia, and Kuwait. Some are built on revenue brought in by raw materials, while others are not.[22]

Belarus has had a targeted national development fund since 2005, drawn from revenue appropriated from highly profitable firms based on their yearly results. The list of firms and the amount appropriated are set each year. In 2020, 40 state-owned enterprises redirected part of their earnings to the fund, and the primary contribution, which was made by the Belarusian Potash Company, made it raw materials-based. However, the fact that contributions are made by state-owned enterprises unrelated to raw materials weakens their incentive to boost productivity. The fund also receives foreign-denominated contributions earned by selling state-owned shares to foreign investors.

Thus, state capitalism in Belarus relies on market tools, like banks with foreign capital and private firms, as well as on their less market-based counterparts: state-owned enterprises, state banks, the Development Bank, and the national development fund. The general mechanism used to operate those levers is often administrative command, and that approach, especially applied to state-owned firms, manifests itself by laying out goals, directing lending, providing financial support, and exerting administrative pressure. While it does offer a short-term boost, over the long term it leads to gradually weakened initiative and growing overheads.

CHAPTER 2

PITFALLS FACING BELARUS' ECONOMY

The past decade in Belarus have seen state capitalism bumping up against barriers to economic growth. Beginning in 2012 growth began to lag behind the global average, and in 2012 and 2013 it was lower than in Russia. In 2015 it dropped to -3.9% for the first time since the 1990s, and it continued falling in 2016 to -2.6%. In 2017 – 2019 economic growth has recovered, but not higher than world average (see Table 2)

Looking back, current estimates point to investment as the primary driver of the fast growth experienced in the past. The IMF holds factors of production responsible for 70% (of which capital created 55% and labour 45%) of growth in output, while productivity came in at around 23%.[23] Other calculations estimate the average contribution of capital to growth from 2006 to 2012 to be 98.3%, accompanied by capacity utilization at 8.3%, labour at -5.3%, and productivity at -1.4%.[24]

However, the impact of investment on GDP growth has waned. While in 2006 each rouble of investment accounted for 0.39 roubles of growth, in 2007 that number dropped to 0.32, in 2010 to 0.23, in 2011 to 0.15, and in 2012–2019 to 0.03–0.05. That trend can be pinned on the poor return offered by investments in social and cultural projects.

The economic downturn can be explained by taking a closer look at the pitfalls facing Belarusian state capitalism.

The 'financing gap' pitfall

The financing gap in the Belarusian economy is defined by two related statistics: inflation, and a deficit in the balance of payments (see Table 2).

Table 2: Average annual macroeconomic statistics for Belarus, %[25] [26]

	1996-2000	2001-2005	2006-2010	2011-2015	2016-2019	2017	2018	2019
GDP growth	6.3	7.5	7.3	1.2	1.1	2.5	3.1	1.2
GDP growth, global	3.7	3.6	3.5	3.6	3.4	3.5	3.6	3.5
GDP growth, Russia	1.8	6.1	3.7	1.9	1.5	1.8	2.5	1.3
Growth in the consumer price index	128.5	25.7	10.4	35.0	6.7	4.6	5.6	4.7
Current account deficit to GDP	-4.1	-2.3	-9.3	-6.3	-1.7	-3.4	0.04	-1.9
Gross external debt to GDP	15.8	22.5	33.4	51.6	44.2	45.6	42.2	42.0
Share of consumption in GDP	78.0	77.1	70.5	64.2	71.4[27]	71.3	70.1	-
Share of investment in GDP	25.2	25.6	28.9	35.1	27.9[28]	28.5	28.4	-
Share of net exports of goods and services in GDP	-4.1	-2.2	-8.6	-0.1	0.5[29]	0.2	1.5	-

1) Inflationary pressure

The internal financing that drove fast-paced growth in the 1990s and 2000s was in many ways emission-based and inflationary. Creating money in an economy featuring a high velocity of money pushes consumer prices higher by channeling that money toward consumption. In underdeveloped financial markets, newly created money also flows toward accessible forms of saving (consumer durables, foreign currency), raising prices and affecting exchange rates. As a result, the inflation experienced in Belarus has been extraordinarily high and long-lasting. For example, from 2005 to May 2014 the consumer price index in Belarus grew 570%. Over the same period the number for Ukraine was 250%, for Russia 230%, for Kazakhstan 220%, for Lithuania 140%, for Poland and the UK 130%, and for the US and the Eurozone 120%.

Long-term inflation has had a progressive, negative effect on the competitiveness of the Belarusian economy for a number of reasons.

A) Inflationary pressure makes it expensive to obtain loans. Interest rates that stay high lead to losses for, and may even halt the operations of, businesses, as the problems building up at the macro level create a toxic situation at the micro level: the past few years have seen rates exceeding 30% and sales margins at around 10%, pushing businesses into bankruptcy. For example, over the first three quarters of 2014, the number of businesses reporting losses grew by a factor of 1.5, with fully a third of manufacturers operating at a loss as of October 1, 2014.

B) Long-term inflationary pressure entrenches inflationary expectations, strengthens dollarization, provides the basis for strange business models (for example, construction sharing that passes inflationary risks on to the apartment buyer), and narrows the list of options for investment planning.

C) Continually creating money over a long period of time exposes banks to risk. Each additional emission has a trickle-down effect in the banking sector that both pushes inflation higher and intensifies systemic risks for banks.

In 2015, the National Bank changed its anti-inflation policy to a monetary regime targeting the expansive money supply. As a result, lending activity slowed: growth in the demand for bank loans dropped to 1% in January–May 2015 from 8% over the same period in 2014. Monetary measures alone, however, do not suffice to hold back inflation in Belarus; they are most effective in market economies where competitive markets already been developed. In markets with monopolies and oligopolies (private or state-owned), regulating prices from the side of the monopolists and government distorts them. With that in mind, deregulating prices and engendering competition are the best non-monetary ways forward. The latter also includes combating cartels and setting fair prices, subject to major changes only as dictated by supply and demand.

Inflation in Belarus has also accelerated currency devaluation that in the last few years has been both protracted and drastic. From 2005 to May 2014 the Belarusian rouble dropped 370% against the dollar. Over that same period the Ukrainian hryvnia dropped 122%, the Kazakhstani tenge dropped 40%, the Russian rouble and the British pound dropped 11%, and the euro dropped 1%; the Chinese yuan grew by 25%. Devaluation boosts prices by making imported goods more expensive and increasing demand for exports, driving domestic production and pushing salaries and domestic prices higher. The coefficient for the effect that devaluation had on inflation in Belarus in 2014 was 0.6–0.64.[30] Reducing the value of the Belarusian rouble by 1% led to a 0.6% boost in consumer prices and a 0.64% boost in producer prices for industrial commodities with a delay of three to six months. In 2015, that coefficient dropped to 0.3 due to the effect of devaluation and inflation in Russia.

Governments tend to prefer an inflationary policy that features a more stable exchange rate. Deciding between a floating or fixed rate depends on a number of factors, but in Belarus the key determinant is whether the monetary authority has the currency reserves and discipline to stick to a fixed exchange rate[31] Sometimes it is easier to let it float.

That's exactly what happened in recent years. A floating exchange rate of the Belarusian rouble (*de facto* following Russian rouble and oil prices) became a relatively stable anchor for inflation. In 2016-2019, the consumer price index dropped to its lowest in the monetary history of Belarus' single-digit parameter. In 2017 and 2019 it was even lower than 5%. On the other hand, monetary targeting and financial stability were the price paid for the low economic growth in the state capitalism model of Belarus.

2) Debt overhang

The external financing coming into the Belarusian economy, and particularly a current account deficit exceeding the threshold of 3–5%, are primarily driven by foreign loans. The inflow of foreign direct investment is limited by the restraints in place on privatization and the investment risks that have accumulated. Even the investment that has come in over the past few years has primarily (more than 90%) been from existing investors reinvesting their earnings. Reducing the current account deficit by reining in consumer and industrial demand for imports would slow growth in living standards among the populace, as well as the country's economy.

External state loans have also built up a debt overhang that saw, for example, 25.4% of foreign-denominated earnings from exports of goods and services in 2014 go toward servicing gross external debt (up from 12.8% in 2012). Slow economic growth over the long term could make it tough to refinance any more loans which are taken, and, considering the medium-term peak payments for foreign-denominated state debt, more external state borrowing (and providing state guarantees) is only feasible in the case of Belarus for refinancing old debt. And even in that case, recession could push the ratio of aggregate external debt to GDP much higher.

It is important to note that access to refinancing is generally linked both to economic development and to non-economic factors like overall confidence in the borrower. Russia had problems in 1991 refinancing a debt that came to 12% of GDP, while Ireland and Luxembourg continue to borrow, even with existing debt which exceeds GDP several times over. The problems that developing countries have in refinancing external debt are therefore of particular interest.

A) Background problems with refinancing (default, or the inability or unwillingness to make debt payments). Developing countries see refinancing problems start to occur on average when external debt reaches 69.3% of GDP.[32] Most often (in 32.3% of instances) they happen when external debt ranges from 41–60% of GDP, while in 19.4% of cases it is when external debt is below 40% of GDP, 16% when it is between 61–80%, 16% when it is between 81–100%, and 16% when it exceeds 100%. The threshold for when a country starts to have problems refinancing external debt can therefore be said, with a high degree of accuracy, to be when existing debt is around 60% of GDP. The ceiling, similarly, seems to be 100%.

B) Fallout following default. The main consequences of default are a drop in investor confidence, a lowered sovereign credit rating, and temporary exclusion from international financial markets. Carmen Reinhart and Kenneth Rogoff looked at 169 defaults from 1946 to 2008 and found that it takes countries three years on average to move past defaults (begin to attract foreign loans again).[33] Interestingly, that period seems to be shrinking: from 1800 to 1945 it took countries an average of six years to get past 127 defaults. It is also worth remembering that defaults have on occasion led to war. For example, there were wars between the UK and Egypt in 1882, the UK and Turkey in 1876, the US and Venezuela in the middle of the 1890s, and the US and Haiti in 1915. The primary objective in each of those cases was to establish military control over customs in order to collect currency as payment for foreign debt.

And so, having built up inflation linked to money creation and external debt, state capitalism in Belarus has fallen into the financing deficit pitfall. Considering that approximately half of GDP in Belarus is created by the private sector, the country's financing deficit is even holding back the natural restructuring process and endangering its long-term health. As a result, the goal of state capitalism in Belarus, aimed as it is at growth, becomes avoiding economic contraction, rather than driving its development.

Given that the primary source of the financing deficit facing the Belarusian economy is the state capitalism system, opening up the economy to foreign capital and stimulating private investment is the way out of this pitfall.

The 'conflict neighbors' pitfall

The term 'conflict neighbors' was coined by Paul Collier to describe how countries surrounded by neighbors in conflict fall into the long-term trap of inhibited economic growth.[34] His study showed that, on average, countries benefit from the economic growth of their neighbors: each point of growth adds 0.4% to the GDP of neighboring countries, though for African countries that number is 0.2%, and for non-African countries it is 0.7%. Political crisis in a country also results in economic losses, both for it, and for its neighbors, totalling an average of 100 billion dollars. The origin of political conflict was also proven to be slow economic growth or contraction in many instances. For example, five years of non-existent economic growth leads to political crisis and civil war in 14% of cases. Each point of growth or contraction improves or lowers the odds of a political crisis occurring. If an economy contracts by 3%, for instance, the likelihood of a crisis happening rises to more than 16%. It was also shown that the longer an economy contracts, the longer it takes to dig itself out of the resulting political crisis. A crisis that culminates in civil war lasts an average of around five years, and countries that go through a civil war have a 50% chance of experiencing another one within the next decade. Economies suffering from civil war contract by an average of 2.3% per year, pulling their neighbors down with them.

The results of Collier's study have an analogy in the Russian-Ukrainian conflict, the civil war in Ukraine, the 2014–2015 recession and the 2016-2019 slow recovery in Russia, and their impact on the Belarusian economy (see Illustration 1). Given the territorial losses suffered by Ukraine, as well as the human cost of the conflict, a fast resolution to the bilateral conflict looks anything but likely. Taking into account the consequences of 2020's coronavirus, it's hard to make predictions as to when Russia will return to growth. While prognoses differ, they share a similar trend: for each point Russian GDP contracts, estimates concur that Belarusian GDP will lose 0.6% of growth thanks to the net-export effect.[35]

Before moving on, it is important to note that Russia and Ukraine are not simply neighbors of Belarus; they are its primary trade and investment partners (Illustration 2). And they have stayed like this through the years, despite their economic recessions or recoveries (if we combine the two illustrations).

Logically speaking, there are two ways out of this pitfall for the Belarusian economy: reorientation towards the domestic market, or diversifying into other foreign markets.

1) Reorienting the economy from foreign markets to the domestic market

While this may be a tempting solution, from January to March 2015, the share of Belarusian sales in the domestic retail market came to 68.9%. For foodstuffs that number was higher, at 81.6%, and for non-foodstuffs it was 50.9%. The domestic market is simply not capable of completely replacing the volume of sales lost in foreign markets without increasing capacity.

Illustration 1. Growth of real GDP in Russia and Ukraine, %, between 2011 and 2019.[36]

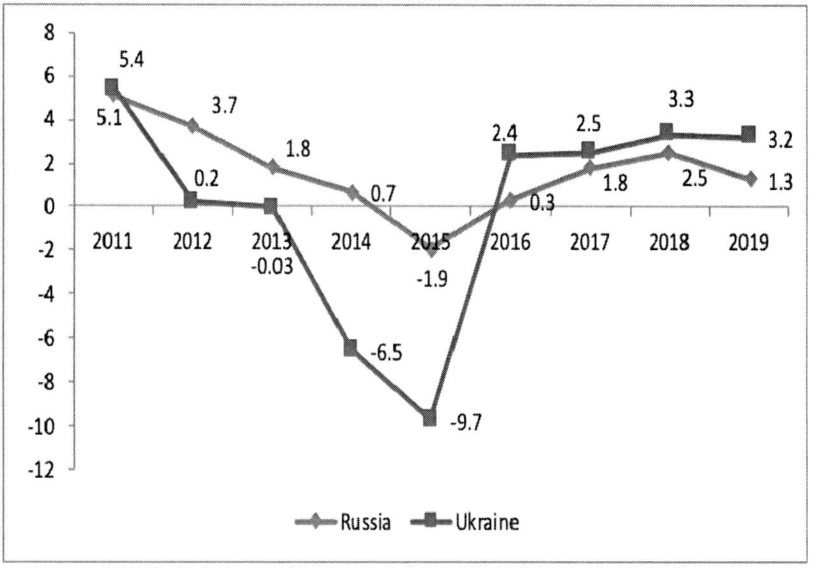

Illustration 2. Russian and Ukrainian exports from, imports to, and foreign direct investment in, Belarus, % of total, 2011–2019.[37]

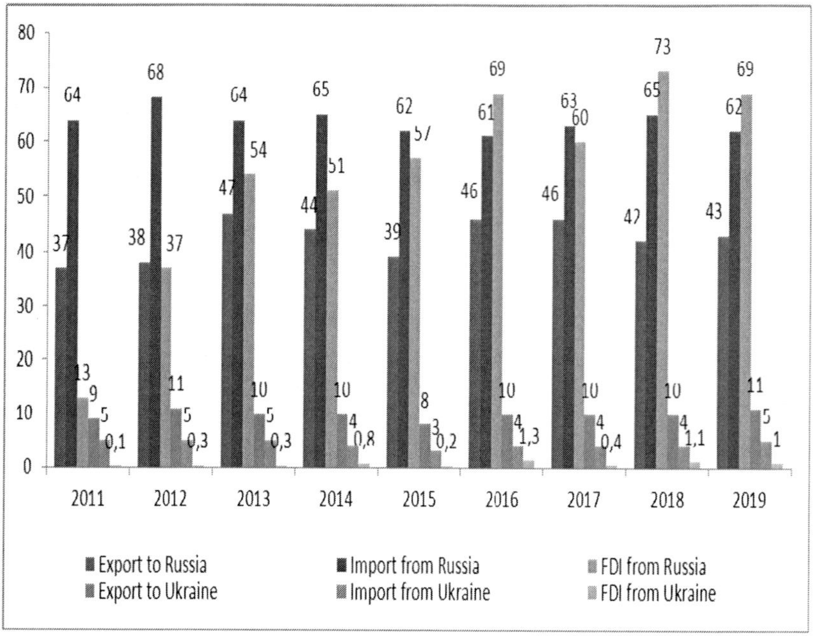

Generally speaking, a reorientation toward domestic markets is generally part of a temporary import substitution strategy geared towards protecting from external competition.

The main argument in favor of import substitution is the need to temporarily shelter high-potential industries or companies from competition. However, in that case, the sheltered industry has to use that opportunity to outpace the development of its foreign competitors (by cutting production costs faster, for example), coming out the other side having made up most of the ground separating them. Developing countries often point to examples where developed countries employed import substitution (the US, Germany, and Japan in the 19th and 20th centuries) to, in their opinion, distance themselves from developing countries over the long term.[38]

Opponents of import substitution bring up the difficulty of deciding which prioritized industries should be protected.[39] Often the obvious choice for the government is looked at askance by private businesses that have invested elsewhere. At that point, the industry is prioritized by the administration, and a temporary import substitution policy becomes permanent. Inflation is also a result of import substitution, as prices for both imported goods (thanks to new protective measures) and domestic goods rise. When that happens, national manufacturers often lower the prices they charge in foreign markets and compensate for the lost revenue by boosting them domestically.

2) Diversification of foreign markets

The focus that Belarusian exports have fixed in the last few years on Russia and Ukraine has less to do with left-over post-Soviet relationships and more to do with their lack of competitiveness and lagging technological development. Belarus' concentration on its largest export market, Russia, has grown in recent years: from 37% of total exports in 2011 to 39% in 2015, and to 43% in 2019. Imports are even more concentrated on Russia. During the last decade, imports from Russia to Belarus stayed more or less at the same level: 64% of total imports in 2011, and 62% in 2015 and 2019.[40]

The problems Russia and Ukraine experienced in 2014–2015 have limited Belarus' export options. That would logically encourage a switch to other markets, but there Belarusian exports are less competitive. The situation is exacerbated by the lack of innovation in Belarusian exports. For example, the country's exporters (the Minsk Automobile Plant, the Minsk Tractor Works) do not have research centers abroad that they can lean on for market analysis and forecasts, to learn about customer needs, and to tweak technology and manufacturing. Competitors like John Deer and MAN have R&D centers in Germany (100 employees), France (120 employees), China, India, and the US. A systemic solution to the problem would be to move from a resource-based economic model to an investment-based model by attracting foreign direct investment, and from there creating a domestic culture of innovation.

The 'conflict neighbor' pitfall often centers on the medium term, with a likelihood of repeat occurrences in the long term, given that long periods of poor economic growth can lead to social unrest. The best way out of this trap for Belarus is to attract foreign direct investment in export companies focusing on highly competitive and high-tech markets.

The 'middle-income' pitfall

The last few years in Belarus have seen the salaries and well-being of the populace grow. Both the rising cost of labour resources on the one hand, and delayed development of innovation, institutions, and markets, on the other, have sapped the country's competitiveness, as compared to others with lower levels of income or better tech. As a result, Belarus is getting dangerously close to the 'middle-income' pitfall, also called the 'development pitfall' or 'middle-income trap' – term introduced by the World Bank economists I. Gill, and H. Kharas. [41]

The 'middle-income' pitfall occurs when rising salaries no longer lead to country-wide development, as measured by GDP per capita (GNI per capita, Atlas), and the country finds itself trapped on a par with other middle-income countries. The borders of the 'middle-income' pitfall start from 1006 dollars and rise to 12235 dollars of GNI per capita.[42] Others use nominal GDP per capita to estimate the 'middle-income trap' within the limits of 10000 dollars to 15000 dollars,[43] or real GDP per capita (purchasing power parity) from 5000 dollars to 10000 dollars.[44] There is also a method to compare developing countries' GDP per capital with the same indicator as the US, and to use it as the share from 5% to 45% to make conclusions about the pitfall.[45]

Using Atlas methodology, it was found out that Belarus fell into the 'middle-income' pitfall after its independence, and has been there for almost three decades. In 2007, Belarus moved from the group of lower middle-income countries to the group of upper middle-income countries with GNI per capita of more than 3956 dollars. But the country didn't go out and reverse the exit in 2014, instead staying in this upper level trap for over ten years already.[46] Of the other countries which fell into the 'middle-income' pitfall in the period from 1989 till 2016, 39 out of 55 countries have been there for more than five years, and 15 out of 55 countries for more than 20 years. The cases of Russia, Croatia, and Equatorial Guinea prove that countries can go back to the 'middle-income' trap, even if they have left it previously.[47]

There are several reasons why Belarus is trapped in the 'middle-income' pitfall.

1) An export-oriented economy

From 2009 to 2018, 31.3% of manufactured goods and services were exported, with that number climbing to 36.6% for 2016, and 36.1% in

2018.[48] At the same time, the rising cost of labour resources has cut into profits and sabotaged Belarusian competitiveness, as compared to countries coupling similar technology with cheaper labour. More importantly, however, those countries themselves are undergoing structural reforms, improving their markets, and developing their institutions, with the effect of entrenching their competitiveness. For example, China's openness and reform policy has pushed its share of global manufacturing from 3–5% in 1990–1995 to 22% in 2013, and to 28% in 2018, while Chinese exports as a percentage of the global total have gone from 1–2% in 1990–1995 to 12% in 2013, and to 17% in 2018.

2) Fading innovation

A lack of spending on research and development, innovation funds that are sometimes not used for their intended purpose, and an overall lack of stimulus for the development of innovation, keep Belarusian exporters from focusing on reducing costs and boosting quality in an effort to improve their competitiveness. For example, the share of expenses devoted to R&D by Belarusian exporters (the Minsk Tractor Works, BelAZ) is several times lower than that of their competitors (John Deer, Caterpillar). In absolute dollar terms, they are outspent thousands of times over. Moreover, Belarusian companies invest in imported technology, while their foreign competitors invest in their own technology. Firms in Belarus purchase high-quality, if imported, equipment that needs to be updated 5–10 years later, meaning that they have to spend the money again to purchase foreign tech. That all intensifies the Belarusian race to improve on old technology, and leaves no room for companies to create new, cutting-edge technology of their own. Technological progress, in short, stalls. The level of R&D expenditures to GDP is rather low. It declined from 0.96% in 2007 to 0.49% in 2015 and increased to 0.6% in 2018.[49]

The situation with innovation in Belarus has also devalued how people look at research and scientists, by chronically underfunding them and leaving their skills unneeded and unwanted. Young doctors of science in Belarus are few and far between. In 2011 and 2012, there was not a single one in the country under the age of 29.[50]

The IT industry's popularity in Belarus neither compensates for the lack of innovation in the real sector, nor contributes to overall labour productivity. Instead, the flow of qualified workers moving to IT from the manufacturing industry sacrifices productivity in the latter without a corresponding boost for the former. But IT, as a self-sufficient and export-oriented industry (separated from the rest of the economy), provides a rather successful case in Belarus. In 2017, new legislature reloaded High-Tech Park with new tax benefits and state guarantees. As a result, in 2019, the IT sector contributed 6.5% to GDP, and 5.2% to total exports of goods and services.

Recent national and global trends in IT provide controversial arguments. On the one hand, the IT industry punches below its weight when calculating GDP, thanks to the relatively cheap consumer services it provides; on the other hand, it clearly punches above its weight in the financial market. A perfect example is Facebook's purchase, for 1 billion dollars, of a company boasting all of 13 employees and no revenue to date. Or look at Facebook's purchase of WhatsApp for 22 billion dollars after it had only totalled 10 million dollars in revenue. J. Haskel and S. Westlake explain in their book *Capitalism without Capital*, that it's all because of the rise of the intangible economy.[51] Nowadays, the cost of branding, marketing, training, and corporate culture, is higher than the cost of equipment, buildings, cars, and warehouses.

It's necessary to add, that development in IT often serves to crowd out the production and consumption of traditional resources and goods which make up GDP, by, for instance, replacing books, tape recorders, televisions, games, mail, and so on with their electronic equivalents. In short, migrating innovation out of real life and into its virtual counterpart is in some ways fake progress which wastes time, money, and human resources that would be better spent in the real sector. Instead of technology that lets us better exchange information, messages, and pictures, we could have science fiction brought to life: flying saucers, mass interplanetary tourism, and more. It's mentioned by the two Nobel Laureates, Abhijit Banerjee and Esther Duflo, in their book *Good Economics for Hard Times*, that if people work instead of spending time on the internet, then GDP could rise more than 30%.[52]

3) Low labour productivity

In Belarus, salary growth over the long term exceeds labour productivity growth multiple times over. For example, from 2000 to 2014, real wages grew 4.8 times, while productivity only grew 2.2 times. From 2010 to 2014, real wages grew 45%; productivity was held to only 14% growth.

Admittedly, labour productivity in Belarusian state-owned firms is lower than in their private and foreign competitors. In 2013, revenue per employee at the joint venture MAN factory was 360,000 dollars, compared to 64,300 dollars at the Minsk Automobile Plant (6 times higher); at John Deer it was 11 times higher compared to the Minsk Tractor Works; at the foreign-owned Olivaria Brewery it was 190,700 dollars, compared to 85,000 dollars at state-owned Krinitsa (half as much); at private Santa Bremor it was 115,900 dollars compared to 83,700 dollars at state-owned Belryba. It is worth noting that the difference in productivity goes beyond technology, a metric according to which state enterprises are comparable to their competitors after modernization; different management systems (manual versus corporate, for instance) explain the difference.

Belarus can therefore get away from the 'middle-income' pitfall by utilizing systemic and operational measures.

A) Systemic measures, which wield a long-term effect include: altering the country's economy structure, accelerating innovative development, and taking steps to boost labour productivity, primarily in state-owned firms. Management systems could be improved, for example, by implementing IT in the manufacturing industry. The necessity of maintaining living standards for Belarusians makes it imperative to compete with other countries for international capital by improving the institutional and entrepreneurial environment, rather than cutting labour costs.

B) Operational measures which enlarge the labour pool in the short term, include: pension reform, getting more women and disabled people into the economy, liberalizing immigration policy, and reducing prison sentences (for example, for non-violent crimes).

The 'social burden' pitfall

The government, with its limited resources, is torn between satisfying the country's growing social needs and solving its economic problems. It generally chooses to prioritize the former at the cost of economic growth.

This high level of social spending, coupled with a resource deficit and growing wages, is calling into question whether the social welfare system will be financed in the future by the government, the people, or other sources of income. At the same time, a population that has grown accustomed to today's level of income and social benefits being subsidized by the government, expects more of the same.

It is important to also note that the purchasing power of wages in Belarus is higher than its face value in dollars. That can be explained by the partial subsidies the government provides for consumer prices, utilities, and social services. While nominal wages in Belarus are lower, for example, than in Russia and Kazakhstan, in terms of purchasing power parity they have been higher in recent years than in Kazakhstan.

The growth in, and level of, salaries in Belarus should be juxtaposed with the approaches taken by other countries, for example, to financing utilities or a number of other social expenses aimed at boosting the national economy's competitiveness.

1) Utilities

In 2015, the government provided a utility subsidy of nearly 70%, and there are plenty of counter-arguments to the impending elimination of cross subsidies.

First, and given the state monopoly in this area which leaves consumers bereft of choices when it comes to which utilities they use and pay for, the key issue is to control expenses, and therefore rates.

Second, raising rates would increase the percentage of private expenses taken up by utilities. In the first quarter of 2015, utilities accounted for 6.9% of household expenses in Belarus. By way of comparison, in 2012 that number was 6.8% in Russia and 9.9% on average in Europe, with the lowest being 3.5% in Finland and the highest being 14% in Slovakia.[53] In other words, completely eliminating cross subsidies in Belarus would be justified, if it were to occur in the context of an increase in private earnings.

Third, utility rates are included in the consumer price index, so raising them would have a trickle-down effect that pushes inflation higher across the entire economy. Doing so, therefore, needs to be gradual in an effort to avoid an inflationary shock.

2) Social support

Social expenditures on, for example, supporting families, are higher in Belarus than in other countries. For instance, paid maternity leave in Belarus is three years, while in Russia it is 1.5 years and in Kazakhstan it is 1 year. The one-time grant given in Belarus at childbirth is 961 dollars for the first child, and 1345 dollars for all following children. In Russia it is 261 dollars, in Poland it is 266 dollars, and in Lithuania it is 469 dollars.

In Kazakhstan, parents are paid 319 dollars for each of their first three children, receiving 532 dollars for all subsequent children. In 2015, Belarus introduced family capital of 10,000 dollars, made available after the birth of third and following children. In Russia, maternity capital comes to 8,160 dollars, while there is no state-sponsored maternity capital system in Kazakhstan, Poland, or Lithuania.

It is also important to note that the number of disabled people is growing, as compared to the rest of the population. For example, the Economy Research Institute forecasts that the ratio of disabled to able people will be 0.907 in 2030 (in 2015 it was 0.705). That highlights the necessity of streamlining entitlements, for example, by moving from universal to targeted support.

There is no need to limit the search for ways in which social spending can be financed to some sort of split between the government and consumers—business could also prove to be an important source. However, social spending is usually seen in the business world as a burden imposed by the government in the form of a minimum wage, educational standards, medical standards, and more. In the 1990s and 2000s, the business model in vogue was to minimize social expenditures by manufacturing in countries with the lowest social requirements and standards: China, Vietnam, Bangladesh, and other Asian countries, for instance.

Since 2010, a new model has appeared whereby meeting, and even exceeding, social standards is profitable for businesses, as Michael Porter put it.[54] For example, considering that physical and mental wear and tear affects both technology and people, companies have been investing both in their technology and their human resources. Businesses benefit when their employees gain new skills, are physically and mentally healthy, and spend their energy on their work without being distracted by social issues. Another example is a telecom company that offers free computer courses for the elderly, boosting demand for its services in the process.

In Belarus, one strategy for privately owned construction companies is to build kindergartens into their new apartment complexes and hand them over to the local authorities, thereby adding to the incentive to buy their apartments. The cost of building the kindergartens is even built into the price of the apartments. Another example is when companies build roads to their shopping centers, business centers, and entertainment complexes. All of that goes back to a business model focused on stimulating demand for goods and services, rather than charity paid by business to finance the state's social infrastructure.

Ultimately, one way out of the social spending pitfall (besides wholesale welfare reform) is a public-private partnership that is both mutually beneficial and voluntary, a qualification without which it would drag business into an unprofitable social sphere and come to nothing. Most practical would be the creation of a fund supported by private, state, and international capital, that could be used to finance the public-private partnerships' social projects (by offering targeted business loans at discounted rates, for instance).

The 'mastering change' pitfall

The system by which the Belarusian state manages the economy does not completely correspond to changing industry and ownership structures, or match up with global approaches to management and control. The difficulty and complexity of the different economic processes in play, the intertwining interests of a variety of entities, and the immense weight of data, as well as analytical and statistical information, make it impossible to centrally formulate standardized management solutions and get them to the actors themselves. Changes in the national and global economies are outpacing the changes made to Belarusian governance, pushing state capitalism toward the 'mastering change' pitfall. That pitfall is when the management apparatus holds less and less influence over the system under it, and a system changing and growing more complex by the day creeps out from under its control and toward independence.

1) Changes in industry and ownership structure

1.1) Industries. The structure of the Belarusian economy has seen the growth of a services sector that began all the way back when it began functioning independently. In 1990, it was responsible for 29% of GDP compared to 69% for manufacturing. By 2000, services were up to 38.6% and manufacturing had fallen to 48.7%. In 2013, the two were roughly equal: 44.8% for services and 44.9% for manufacturing. And in 2019, the service sector was 48.8% of GDP, while the production sector was only 38.1%. When it comes to individual sectors, industry and construction have been falling, with transport and communication services picking up the slack (see Table 3). The current system of regulations focuses primarily on businesses in the manufacturing industry even though giants like the Minsk Automobile Plant, the Minsk Tractor Works, Belarusian

Steel Works, and Grodno Azot are responsible for significantly less than small and medium businesses (25%).

Table 3: Industry breakdown of the Belarusian economy, average yearly % of GDP[55]

Industry	1996-2000	2001-2005	2006-2010	2011-2015	2016-2018
Manufacturing	28.4	26.8	26.2	23.0	21.0
Agriculture and forestry	13.1	9.3	8.5	7.3	7.0
Construction	5.6	6.2	8.9	8.4	5.4
Transportation and communications	10.8	9.8	8.5	8.8	10.9
Trade and food services	8.6	9.8	10.9	13.8	11.3

1.2) Ownership forms. Organizations with non-state forms of ownership influence the country's social and economic growth just as much as their state-owned counterparts. While in 1990 there were almost no privately owned companies in Belarus, in 2013 companies in which the government did not hold a stake created around half of GDP, just as much as the public sector did, and in 2019 the private sector was bigger than the public. In 2019, the private sector was also responsible for 67.5% of exports of goods, 72.6% of exports of services and 56.6% of employment. Regulation that goes beyond state-owned enterprises (by laying out and monitoring goals) to all forms of economic relationships (via the regulatory framework and regular monitoring) is needed.

2) Changes in management and the control exerted over corporations

2.1) Management. Manual management, even with modernized technology, keeps many Belarusian state-owned enterprises from competing with companies equipped with similar technology, but different management models. The administrative resource in state-owned enterprises is oriented towards complying with existing rules and regulations, as well as executing the instructions and assignments that are handed down, sometimes to the detriment of profits. Incentives are distorted, initiative is fettered, and growth in labour productivity is suppressed.

International companies generally have a corporate governance structure: an advisory board, a board of directors, and an assembly of shareholders, all with strictly delineated functions, authorities, and responsibilities. However, they all share a common goal—profit and dividends—that filters down as the motivation for each individual employee and manager with the freedom to initiate as they see fit within the authority they have been granted.

2.2) Control and monitoring. The monitoring system in place in state-owned enterprises in Belarus is limited in its effectiveness. With growth in the size and complexity of the economy, even simple transactions demonstrate the need for more monitoring. However, the more steps which are taken to keep a closer eye on the situation, the more minor violations are found, making closer monitoring necessary, which finds even more minor violations—and sometimes violations are all treated in the same way, no matter how minor. Instead of mobilization, an opposing effect is observed, where more and more managers avoid carrying out even current solutions, let alone taking on major economic risk. Sometimes the mistakes that are discovered, are covered up instead of being quickly and quietly resolved, leading to other mistakes and making the problems deeper. In an effort to monitor and double-check everything, even the monitors themselves have to be monitored to keep them from abusing their positions.

International corporations accept missed deadlines and going over budget as normal commercial risks which they can insure against by building penalties into contracts or, if all else fails, resolving the situation in court. For example, of the 717 projects begun in the UK from 1992 to 2012 as part of public-private partnerships where the state was the client, only 69% of contracts were finished on time at an appropriate level of quality, and only 65% were finished under budget. Problems were handled contractually between the parties, or in arbitration, with law enforcement never getting involved.

Andy Grove, President and CEO of Intel, eloquently described the way out of the 'mastering management' pitfall in his book *Only the paranoid survive.*[56] Paranoid managers are those who always remember that the world is changing around them. They continually gather information from those below them, learn, think strategically, and react quickly. In this regard, the series of books by Ichak Adizes on how to master changes is also rather useful.[57][58]

For Belarus, getting out of this pitfall means decentralizing state regulation of the economy as well as strengthening and promoting independence and material incentives for state institutions to bring in results-oriented professionals. Better information, in addition to more openness and transparency, is critical, as are keeping decision-making out of the hands of individuals, engendering trust, and building respect. Authority has to be delegated to ministries, departments, and sections, in keeping with the principle that simpler problems can be solved farther down the food chain. Dividing up the regulatory and economic functions of state agencies needs to happen, putting ministries in charge of industries and more general areas without responsibility for the economy on the micro level.

The state would be wise to deprioritize the letter of the law when it comes to monitoring compliance with the rules governing business (something that is undoubtedly important in an institutional economy). As it sets up institutions and oversees the development of the economy, most important is for Belarus to ensure currency and financial stability by prioritizing tax- and currency-related crimes (though punishing them cannot be used as a means to other ends). Relaxing control, especially over small and medium businesses, would create space for them to experiment, try new approaches and methods, test new suppliers and clients, and breathe life into the economy. Once changes have been made to economic structures, control can be adapted to those new forms, and fully reinstated.

The 'resource curse' pitfall

This trap occurs when the economy, and in particular exports, is based on preferential access to raw materials, forcing it into dependence on external factors (global prices, foreign trading partners, competitors) and pushing industries not based on raw materials into the background. Favorable conditions see exports and the economy grow, but digging themselves deeper and deeper into the hole in the process, while economic downturns lead to falling exports, economic growth, and living standards. Free or preferential access to raw materials also saps the state's need for tax revenue and strong institutions. When the economy takes a turn for the worse, and the prices for raw materials drop, institutions and tax revenue are not there to continue stable economic development.

This pitfall is a real and present danger for the Belarusian economy, due to the petrochemical sector's outsized presence, and the Russian factor.

1) The petrochemical sector

The petrochemical industry exploited a period of low crude oil prices and high prices on finished products to boost its share of the country's GDP. In 2009, oil refining and chemical production created 4.7% of GDP; in 2019 they created around 7%. Raw materials also became more of the country's focus when it came to exports. For example, the share of oil, petroleum products, and potash fertilizers in Belarusian exports went from 35% in 2010 to 38% in 2014. And even within that number, oil and petroleum products went from 26% to 30%, while potash fertilizers dropped from 9% to 8%.

Falling global potassium prices in 2013–2014 and oil prices in 2014–2015 (a trend that will most likely be deep and protracted), coupled with a lesser fall in prices for petroleum products, necessitates a new economic structure for Belarus. A fast bounce-back of global oil prices and a return to the old national economic structure are unlikely, and not borne out by a knowledge of history. The average historical oil price (in terms of the dollar's value in 2000) from 1880 to 2004 was 19.61 dollars per barrel.[59] The historic highs enjoyed by the global economy have been a recent phenomenon: in 2010–2014 Brent crude averaged 102 dollars per barrel, creating an unsustainable bubble in the economies of a number of countries. The dramatic drop in oil prices has also had an impact on both production quantities and the financial wellbeing of oil refineries, which are Belarus' largest exports and taxpayers and are in the middle of modernization. In 2013, the share of exports taken up by goods and services provided by Mozyr Oil Refinery and Naftan was 16%.

On the other hand, the impact that dropping crude oil prices have had on the Belarusian oil refinery sector should not be overstated. Prices of crude are correlated with prices of oil refinery goods, so the net profit brought in by oil refineries should remain more or less the same. Efficiency, rather than price changes, is a much heftier driver of profits, and decreased export customs duties have made the biggest difference that the oil price drop has had on the Belarusian refining sector.

2) The Russian factor

Russia's oil-based economic structure, the formation of the Eurasian Economic Space, and the orientation of 43% (as of 2019) of Belarusian exports towards the Russian market make the Russian factor a critical piece of the puzzle. In 2019, oil was responsible for 48% of imports from Russia to Belarus, adding gas pushes that numbered 68%, and adding metals takes the overall share of raw materials to 78%.

Given the Russian rouble's floating rate, the global collapses of oil prices in 2014–2015, and early 2020 were mirrored almost exactly by the exchange rate. The Russian rouble has been *de facto* pegged to the price of oil. Certainly, the plummeting price of oil has not been the only factor exerting downward pressure on the Russian rouble. Countries like Angola, Algeria, Kuwait, Iran, Iraq, and Nigeria, all with higher oil exports to GDP ratio than Russia, saw their currencies devalue less dramatically than the Russian rouble in 2014–2015.

The weakening Russian rouble has a corresponding effect on the competitiveness of Belarusian exports to Russia. Not only that, but the floating Belarusian rouble rate, the fact that the Russian rouble is in the Belarusian currency basket, and the close economic relationship between Belarus and Russia, mean that changing global oil prices affect the value of the Belarusian rouble as well, via currency and trade channels.

All in all, the Belarusian economy's post-Soviet structure, its overbearing focus on the raw materials of the petrochemical and potassium sector, and its close ties to the raw materials-based Russian economy creates the framework for a fall into the 'resource curse' pitfall. Norway is a textbook example of how to get out of that trap, as the oil and gas sector there is responsible for more than 50% of the country's export revenue. Even so, it has maintained stable economic growth—while raw materials and the role they play in exports are an important factor in the country's economic growth, they are not the determining factor. The main difference is that institutions were built in Norway before raw materials were developed on an industrial scale (before the 1970s), making it immune to external shocks today. The way out of the resource curse pitfall, ultimately, means going back to the necessity of institutional reform.

The 'long-term stagnation' pitfall

While the pitfalls that face state capitalism in Belarus, seen above, represent the danger of slowed economic growth in the medium term, falling into the long-term stagnation pit means inhibited growth and lagging economic growth over a longer period of time, analogous to Japan's two lost decades in 1990–2010 as well as the theory of secular stagnation facing the US.[606162] Those examples of poor growth in labour productivity, missing innovation, and a ceiling that prevents further debt-based financing of the economy over the long run, are real, and have definite similarities to the state capitalism pitfalls we have already discussed.

The principle difference is that Belarus, were it to fall into even a medium-term pitfall, and the economic consequence, would fall significantly behind its neighbors, and even the more measured growth of developed countries (see Table 4). This situation of long-term delay was forecasted in 2015,[63] and now becomes reality. One of the reasons is the choice of Russia as an economic anchor for Belarus. Obviously the situation would have been different and more optimistic if the anchor had been the EU or China.

Table 4: Growth in real GDP, 2011–2019[64]

	2011-2019	2019
Global	3.5	3.5
USA	2.3	2.2
EU	1.6	1.6
China	7.3	6.1
Russia	1.7	1.3
Belarus	1.15	1.2

Belarus needs a long-term average growth rate exceeding the average for developing countries, or around 7%, in order to catch up. To simply stay in the group of developing countries it needs to maintain a yearly growth rate of around 5%. Anything less will put the country in danger of falling into the 'long-term stagnation' pitfall.

Three growth options were looked at for the Belarusian economy, and factored against different population growth rates, giving a glimpse of the country's long-term economic growth through the lens of GDP per capita, in purchasing power parity terms. In all, the 2030 GDP per capita was calculated for the following scenarios (see Table 5):

A) Average yearly growth rates of GDP: 1%, 5%, and 7%. The first option corresponds to the average historical growth rate per capita: from 1700 to 2012 the number grew by an average of 0.8% per year, though from 1913 to 2012 that number was 1.6%.[65] As has already been seen, in that case, the Belarusian economy would fall behind faster-growing developing and developed countries. The latter two options represent Belarus' path to catching up to, and overtaking, respectively, those countries.

B) Population change: a reduction of 0.5% per year and maintaining current levels. The former option was discussed in the UN's forecast for 2030, which had the Belarusian population potentially dropping from 9.4 million people in 2013 to 8.5 million in 2030 at a rate of -0.56% per year. The second option—maintaining current levels—has been given impetus by the trend seen in the last few years toward population growth. Over the course of 2014, the population grew by 12,800, more than making up for the 1,900 it lost in 2012.

Table 6: 2030 scenarios for GDP per capita in Belarus in terms of PPP[66]

Yearly GDP growth / Yearly population growth	1%	5%	7%
-0.56%	USD 22,961	USD 44,438	USD 61,244
0%	USD 20,871	USD 40,392	USD 55,667

These scenarios make it possible to calculate reference points for Belarusian growth among developing and developed countries:

1) Yearly GDP growth of 1% and no population loss would leave GDP per capita at 20,871 dollars in 2030, at the level of Kazakhstan in 2011, as well as Russia, Estonia, and Poland in 2009.
2) Yearly GDP growth of 1% and a shrinking population would leave GDP per capita at 22,961 dollars in 2030, at the level of Russia and Lithuania in 2012, Estonia in 2011, and Slovakia in 2007.

3) Yearly GDP growth of 5% and no population loss would leave GDP per capita at 40,392 dollars in 2030, at the level of Germany and Canada in 2011.
4) Yearly GDP growth of 5% and a shrinking population would leave GDP per capita at 44,438 dollars in 2030, at the level of the US in 2000.
5) Yearly GDP growth of 7% and no population loss would leave GDP per capita at 55,667 dollars in 2030, at the level of the UAE in 2011.
6) Yearly GDP growth of 7% and a shrinking population would leave GDP per capita at 61,244 dollars in 2030, at the level of Norway in 2010 and Singapore in 2000.

Ultimately, the long-term stagnation pitfall represents what would happen were the rest of the pitfalls to go uncorrected and lead to poor economic growth. The Belarusian economy would fall behind both developed and developing countries (including its neighbors) over the long run. Avoiding it requires state capitalism to move from a growth-oriented model to a development-oriented model.

PART 2.

"TRANSFORMERS": STORIES OF SUCCESSFUL TRANSITION

CHAPTER 3

ECONOMIC TRANSFORMATION (IN POST-SOVIET, CENTRAL EUROPEAN, AND EASTERN EUROPEAN COUNTRIES)

Both political and economic factors lay at the root of the Soviet economic system's collapse.

The political reasons included ideological aggression, the outsized influence wielded by security agencies, a lack of democracy, and a single-party system.

The economic reasons included little motivation to work, a ban on entrepreneurship as an important element of creative self-expression, an ineffective economic management system, excessive state planning and administrative reallocation of resources, a humiliating lack of needed goods and overproduction of unneeded goods, revenue dependent on energy resources, a preponderance of indirect taxes (excise duties on alcoholic beverages), and high defense spending (accounting for over half the budget of the USSR).

Experts say the main reason for the collapse of the Soviet empire was the long-standing stagnation of its economy and an inability to financially support its satellites.[67][68] By the 1980s, the cost of supporting the Soviet empire had risen beyond 40 billion dollars (of which nearly 10 billion went toward financing Cuba). According to the RAND Corporation, that number was growing by 8.7% each year, significantly outpacing the growth rate of the Soviet economy. The threefold drop in oil prices at the beginning of the 1980s cut into the Soviet Union's primary hard-currency revenue and led to curtailed funding for its allies.

The Soviet Union's reaction to that economic downturn was to increase state spending. The government boosted state investment by buying foreign equipment using state bank loans and foreign debt. The exchange rate was fixed at 0.63 Soviet roubles to the dollar, and prices were strictly regulated. These measures drove economic growth for two years, but in 1989, a ten-year recession set in. The country ultimately collapsed under its weight.

The analysis of the economic transformation experienced by post-Soviet countries focused on 12 of them who were part of the CIS after the collapse of the Soviet Union: Azerbaijan, Armenia, Belarus, Georgia, Kazakhstan, Kyrgyzstan, Moldova, Russia, Tajikistan, Turkmenistan, Uzbekistan, and Ukraine. 14 countries were included for Central and Eastern Europe: Albania, Bulgaria, Hungary, Latvia, Lithuania, Macedonia, Poland, Romania, Slovakia, Croatia, the Czech Republic, and Estonia. The period of structural economic reforms was split into two stages: economic adaptation to a new structure and post-reform development.

Economic adaptation to a new structure

Poland is considered to be a pioneer of reform. It started with stabilization at the macro level by tightening fiscal and monetary policy, reaching an agreement to cancel half (15 billion dollars) of its external debt, and liberalizing prices. That was coupled with institutional transformation that included rapid small-scale privatization and a relatively gradual privatization of big state-owned enterprises, setting up an independent central bank, and transforming public administration. As the Polish deputy prime minister in 1989–1991, Leszek Balcerowicz, put it, a "risky strategy is better than a hopeless one", and reform was nothing if not fast and radical.[69] However, focusing on the reforms themselves without explaining them to the public made the reformers unpopular among lobbyists and employees of state-owned enterprises. Reforms slowed until a second wave in 1997 resulted in a new economic structure and environment.

Hungary is another good story of an early reformer. It established a competitive banking system, a privatization agency, and a crawling pegged exchange rate regime. New laws on bankruptcy, state asset management, accounting, and privatization appeared well ordered, and attracted investment in the public sector. As a result, in the 1990s, Hungary reeled in almost half the foreign direct investment going to Central and East European countries. Small and medium-sized companies growing into relatively large companies with a sense of private ownership were at the core of the economic rebirth.

The Czech Republic was reformed by a relatively small group of academic economists lead by Václav Klaus. They demonstrated what needed to be done, showed how to do it, and logically explained the reforms, step-by-step, to the public so there would be no surprises. Starting with a rapid voucher-based privatization, desubsidization, and deregulation, the Czech Republic radically restructured its government institutions. The country also introduced a fixed exchange rate in the face of IMF recommendations to the contrary, something that provided a much-needed anchor in the midst of pervasive change.

Russia is an example of how reforms can start off well and take a turn for the worse. When the Soviet Union collapsed, it was at the pre-revolution stage: hyperinflation, dropping output, almost no international reserves, and in the middle of a default. Deputy Prime Minister Gaidar and his team (Aven and Chubais) were entrusted with beginning reforms, and they started by liberalizing prices, cutting arms procurement, and beginning local privatization on a small scale, as well as some larger privatizations for a few individuals, liberalizing trade, and converting the rouble. A lack of institutions let reforms get off on the right foot, but later political intervention stopped, and even reversed them. The old-fashioned Russian parliament and influential secret service distanced the reformers from the seat of power, introduced an unusual rouble zone system, regulated energy prices, drove away international financial support, and raised public spending and enterprise subsidies. All that resulted in a rent-seeking economy, instead of one that was market-oriented, competitive, and institutional.

The first stage of adaptation took several years and was accompanied by a drop in real GDP common to all the countries studied. That economic slump meant that reforms not only fixed the problems; they also led to the old economic structure fading away. Growth returned after the new structure was put in place and attained a mobile equilibrium. With that said, each individual economy had its own way of adapting to the new structure, for which reason three indicators were used to establish the framework for a comparative assessment: how long the economic slump was (the adaptation), the depth of the slump, and a comprehensive index used to measure structural reform (see Table 6).

A) The duration of the economic slump is the key indicator of adaptability. The faster a country was able to return to growth, the faster its economy was able to adapt to the new structure and start moving toward development.

B) If countries took an identical period of time to dig themselves out of their slumps, the depths of the slumps themselves were compared.
C) A comprehensive index was calculated in an effort to evaluate each country's progress down the road to reform.

That index was calculated as the average value of metrics used by the European Bank for Reconstruction and Development: privatization of major corporations, privatization of small business, restructured organizations, liberalized prices, trade and currency systems, competition policy, bank reforms, liberalized interest rates, financial markets, non-bank institutions, general infrastructure reform, telecommunications, energy, road development, and water resource usage.

The criteria for those metrics were built on the EBRD methodology with a scale from 1 to 4, with 1 meaning a complete absence of reform, and 4 indicating completed reforms.

Table 6: Comparative evaluation of the adaptability of different countries[70][71][72][73][74]

Country, group	Adaptation period (number of years)	Yearly growth of real GDP during the adaptation period, %	Average comprehensive index of structural reforms over the adaptation period	Coefficient for the correlation between the structural reform index and economic growth
1. Poland	1989-1991 (3)	-6.13	1.88	-0.84
2. Armenia	1991-1993 (3)	-20.76	1.26	-0.37
3. Czech Republic	1989-1992 (4)	-2.97	1.55	-0.31
4. Slovenia	1989-1992 (4)	-5.91	1.64	-0.49
5. Romania	1989-1992 (4)	-8.30	1.14	-0.5
6. Albania	1989-1992 (4)	-8.90	1.12	-0.07
7. Georgia	1991-1994 (4)	-25.55	1.18	0.10
8. Hungary	1989-1993 (5)	-3.68	2.12	-0.18
9. Uzbekistan	1991-1995 (5)	-3.80	1.38	0.26
10. Slovakia	1989-1993 (5)	-5.06	1.62	-0.51
11. Bulgaria	1989-1993 (5)	-5.82	1.42	-0.02
12. Belarus	**1991-1995 (5)**	**-8.10**	**1.35**	**-0.73**
13. Kazakhstan	1991-1995 (5)	-9.26	1.43	0.05
14. Croatia	1989-1993 (5)	-9.90	1.68	-0.22
15. Latvia	1989-1993 (5)	-10.08	1.37	-0.78
16. Kyrgyzstan	1991-1995 (5)	-12.54	1.67	-0.11
17. Serbia	1989-1993 (5)	-15.38	1.48	-0.99

18. Azerbaijan	1991-1995 (5)	-15.58	1.46	-0.16
19. Estonia	1989-1994 (6)	-6.10	1.83	-0.23
20. Russia	1991-1996 (6)	-8.13	1.99	0.17
21. Lithuania	1989-1994 (6)	-9.40	1.48	-0.53
22. Tajikistan	1991-1996 (6)	-13.81	1.28	0.21
23. Moldova	1991-1996 (6)	-14.33	1.67	0.45
24. Macedonia	1989-1995 (7)	-4.60	1.79	0.21
25. Turkmenistan	1991-1997 (7)	-8.92	1.11	-0.28
26. Ukraine	1991-1999 (9)	-9.41	1.73	0.68
CEE	**1989-1993 (5)**	**-6.61**	**1.58**	**-0.47**
CIS	**1991-1996 (6)**	**-9.93**	**1.37**	**0.62**
All countries	**1989-1994 (6)**	**-7.00**	**1.48**	**-0.37**

It would be incorrect to state that the intensiveness of reforms during the adaptation stage influenced the duration or depth of the slump overall. Some countries featured a low coefficient for the correlation between reforms and economic growth: Bulgaria (-0.02), Kazakhstan (0.05), and Albania (-0.07). The rest had a high coefficient. In some cases, it was true that the depth of the slump was related to the intensiveness with which reforms were carried out: for example, Serbia (with a correlation coefficient of -0.99), Poland (-0.84), and Belarus (-0.73).

There were three areas (prices, labour, and capital) where economies differentiated themselves from each other as they adapted to the new structure.

1) Prices. Many countries experienced hyperinflation, lending weight to the critics of reform.[75] The average growth of the consumer price index across the adaptation period from 1989 to 1994 in all countries was 435.8%, though in CEE from 1989 to 1993 it was 195.2%, and in the CIS from 1991 to 1996 it was 1214.8%. Inflation also had some distinct features:

A) A weak banking system was met with high demand for credit resources, though borrowers turned out to be insolvent and banks were forced to stop issuing loans. Central banks printed money to support the banking system, and the lack of accompanying growth in production led to inflation.

B) A lack of currency reserves (for instance, Georgia had currency reserves of 700,000 dollars in 1992, while Armenia had 1.3 million dollars) and experience of managing exchange rates led to devalued national currencies and price hikes.

C) Heavy wear and tear on the main assets leading to a need for modernization, or sometimes even complete replacement, boosted production costs and pushed prices higher.

D) A policy of maintaining low unemployment in an effort to circumvent problems stemming from unemployment and falling living conditions also drove inflation higher.

2) Labour. Bankruptcy, restructuring inefficient state enterprises, curtailing the state's responsibility to provide employment, and boosting labour productivity requirements, led to growth in unemployment. For example, in 1992 unemployment in Poland was 13.3%, and in 1993 it was 21.4% in Bulgaria and 12.2% in Slovakia. A situation arose wherein poorly qualified labour in the private sector was paid more than highly qualified labour in the public sector.

Lost wages and unemployment pushed labour out of those countries, with the largest migrations leaving Uzbekistan in 1993 (20.4% of the entire work force), Georgia in 1992 (16.9%), Hungary in 1991 (10.1%) and 1993 (9%), Estonia in 1993 (5.4%), and the Czech Republic in 1992 (5.1%).

3) Capital. Lost domestic capital was not replaced by foreign capital over the adaptation period, leaving countries like Uzbekistan, Kyrgyzstan, Kazakhstan, and Armenia with a significant capital deficit. The situation was sometimes even intensified by capital flight (especially out of Russia, Ukraine, Romania, and Slovenia). Foreign direct investment took over as the main source of financing for the adapting economies, though it was reserved primarily for CEE: from 1989 to 1994 the region attracted 80% of all the foreign direct investment going to the countries on the list, leaving just 20% for the CIS.[76]

The largest quantity of foreign direct investment went to countries busy privatizing their state-owned enterprises. The coefficient for the correlation between privatizing major companies and influxes of foreign direct investment in Poland was 0.75, while in Hungary and Romania it was 0.7. The coefficient for the correlation between privatizing small businesses and influxes of foreign investment was somewhat lower: 0.64 in Poland and Hungary, 0.5 in Romania. Mass privatization took place in Russia, where more than 89,000 companies were privatized by the end of 1993; in the Czech Republic, where 988 companies were privatized in 1992 followed by another 861 in 1994; Slovenia, where 1543 companies were privatized in 1992; Poland, where 512 companies were privatized; and Slovakia, where 503 companies were privatized.[77]

Privatization was also accompanied by the development of a financial market and an inflow of foreign portfolio investment. The coefficient for the correlation between privatizing major companies and the development of a financial market was 0.78 for all countries, and 0.70 for the correlation between privatizing small companies and the development of a financial market.

Adaptability to a new economic structure depended on the depth of the slump, or, in other words, whether the internal reserves were in place for reform. That helped countries adapt faster and made for a less painful transition to the development stage. The characteristics shared through the adaptation stage were: an inflation spike, mobile labour and financial resources, and an influx of foreign direct investment, primarily in privatization projects.

Developing a new economic structure

The second stage of development featured economic growth within the new structure. However, that does not mean that the structural reforms in those countries were complete; they continued, providing constant adjustments. Different countries also went through reform at different paces depending on their goals, domestic and foreign stimuli, and ability. Some of them—Russia and, more recently, Hungary—reversed reforms by sacrificing them to the idea of nation building. Others, like Georgia, Estonia, and Slovakia, became standard-bearers for new reforms and now boast impressive results. Still more, like Ukraine and Bulgaria, have enjoyed promising, if vulnerable, starts. Finally, countries like Tajikistan and Turkmenistan remain trapped in unreformist logic.

Georgia is an excellent example of a recently successful reformer. Beginning in 2004, it freed business from illegal interference and excessive restraints, blowing the doors off the economy. The Libertarian Minister of Economy, Kakha Bendukidze, then implemented some radical reforms: privatization of electricity generation and distribution networks, agricultural land, seaports, airports, and other infrastructure, in addition to tax amnesty. Georgia opened its sky to all airlines, liberalized its visa policy, opened a domestic pharmaceutical industry, and implemented police reform. The Economic Liberty Act was passed, prohibiting all limitations on currency conversions, opening bank accounts, banning tax increases, and establishing new regulations.

Estonia is another success story of post-reformist innovation, openness, and rapid development. Recent reforms spread through the country's microeconomy based on macroeconomic stability achieved by the currency board. They included tax reform (abolishing a corporate tax on reinvested profits), pension reform, and the introduction of e-government to reduce corruption and improve public services. Estonia privatized its big state-owned enterprises, a process that was admittedly hampered by opposition lobbyists. The lesson here is that reforms should be enacted quickly, with a view toward the big picture, without wasting time on the details, and be built on modern technology.

CEE countries like Hungary and Poland strove to match European standards for economic development. In 1995, Jeffrey Sachs and Andrew Warner came up with three development scenarios and how they would get them to 70% and 90% of average EU income:[78]

Scenario 1: In the case of negligible reform and continued growth in Poland of 3.53% and in Hungary of 1.91%, neither of the two would reach the two milestones.

Scenario 2: In the case of limited reforms, GDP growth of 2.8% in Hungary would have the country reaching the first milestone (70%) in 45 years and the second (90%) in 120 years. Yearly growth of 4.3% would have Poland reaching the first milestone in 65 years and the second in 141 years.

Scenario 3: In the case of active reforms that push growth to 4.6% in Hungary, the first milestone would be reached in 13 years and the second in 23 years.

Poland would take 21 and 31 years to reach the two milestones, respectively, were growth to average 6.1%.

After almost two decades we are in a position to check Sachs and Warner's work. In 2013, Hungary reached 75% of the average EU number (as of 1995), having averaged 2.2% growth, while Poland had reached 79% of it, thanks to 4.1% growth. In real terms, in 2013, Hungary and Poland came in at 40% and 41.5%, respectively, of the average EU level, showing that developing countries can leverage active reform to close the gap standing between them and developed countries faster than would have otherwise been possible.

The comprehensive structural reform index, and average yearly growth in real GDP were used to compare how actively reforms were pursued during the development period (see Table 7).

Table 7: Comparison of structural reform and post-reform development in transitioning countries, 2013[79][80][81][82][83]

Country	Development stage	Changes in the comprehensive reform index in 2014 terms, lower and upper margins	Average growth in real GDP during the development stage	Average growth in real GDP from 2011 to 2013
1. Poland	1992 – 2013	1.88 – 3.66	4.1	2.8
2. Latvia	1994 – 2013	1.37 – 3.61	4.0	4.8
3. Estonia	1995 – 2013	1.83 – 3.61	4.3	4.9
4. Slovakia	1994 – 2013	1.62 – 3.38	4.2	1.9
5. Hungary	1994 – 2013	2.12 – 3.38	2.2	0.6
6. Romania	1993 – 2013	1.14 – 3.33	2.4	2.1
7. Lithuania	1995 – 2013	1.48 – 3.33	4.2	4.3
8. Bulgaria	1994 – 2013	1.42 – 3.22	1.9	1.2
9. Croatia	1994 – 2013	1.68 – 3.22	2.7	-1.1
10. Slovenia	1993 – 2013	1.64 – 3.16	2.7	-1.0
11. Russia	1997 – 2013	1.99 – 3.0	4.0	3.0
12. Macedonia	1996 – 2013	1.79 – 2.83	2.4	1.8
13. Serbia	1994 – 2013	1.48 – 2.72	3.1	1.0
14. Albania	1993 – 2013	1.12 – 2.70	5.6	1.8
15. Georgia	1995 – 2013	1.18 – 2.66	5.8	5.6
16. Armenia	1994 – 2013	1.26 – 2.61	6.8	5.13
17. Moldova	1997 – 2013	1.67 – 2.61	3.5	5.0

18. Ukraine	2000 – 2013	1.73 – 2.61	4.1	2.4
19. Kazakhstan	1996 – 2013	1.43 – 2.55	6.3	6.2
20. Kyrgyzstan	1996 – 2013	1.67 – 2.33	4.7	5.5
21. Azerbaijan	1996 – 2013	1.46 – 2.27	11.1	2.7
22. Tajikistan	1997 - 2013	1.28 – 2.11	7.2	7.4
23. Uzbekistan	1996 – 2013	1.38 – 1.88	6.1	8.2
24. Belarus	**1996 – 2013**	**1.35 – 1.83**	**6.3**	**2.7**
25. Turkmenistan	1998 – 2013	1.11 – 1.27	12.7	12.0
CCE	**1994 – 2013**	**1.58 – 3.24**	**4.1**	**1.9**
CIS	**1997 – 2013**	**1.37 – 2.31**	**5.0**	**5.5**
All countries	**1995 – 2013**	**1.48 – 2.79**	**2.8**	**3.6**

Those numbers show that the structural reforms undergone by CEE on the scale of 1 to 4 average out to 3.24, while the analogous number for the CIS is 2.31. With that said, it would be inaccurate to claim that structural reforms lead necessarily to high long-term growth rates. Poland, Latvia, Estonia, and Slovakia all experienced limited growth over the indicated period while still undergoing active reforms. On the contrary, the correlation between the GDP growth dynamic and the intensity with which reforms were carried out (-0.7) lends itself to the conclusion that slow economic growth stimulated those countries to intensify their structural reforms.

Following that logic, a new wave of reforms should be expected in countries that have seen slowed growth over the past few years (2011–2013), coupled with a lack of structural transformation: Azerbaijan, Albania, Belarus, Macedonia, Serbia, and Ukraine. Russia could also be added to that group, given the fact that fully-fledged structural reforms were never taken to their conclusion, a fact substantiated by the comprehensive reform index and the assessments of Russian economists.[84]

The countries going through the development stage displayed features that were, for the most part, more regional and global than individual: it is important to take into account the impact of the Russian default in 1998, the recovery of 1999–2001, the rise from 2002 to 2007, the global financial crisis in 2008–2009, and its fallout in 2010–2013. Countries were also able to take care of a number of adaptation problems over that longer period, though some were left unresolved.

1) Prices. Inflation slowed significantly (especially in CEE), and some countries (Latvia (2010), Ukraine (2013), and Estonia (2009)) even went into deflation. That was facilitated by the long-term effect of liberalizing prices and trade, as well as primarily fixed exchange-rate policies. Only Albania, Moldova, Poland, Romania, and the Czech Republic went for long periods of time during the development stage with floating currencies; the rest stuck to some sort of fixed exchange rate.

Monetary and fiscal inflation in the transitioning countries expresses itself differently depending on the source. Monetary inflation is less pronounced: the correlation between monetization and inflation was 0.28. The coefficient for the correlation between budget deficits and inflation turned out to be -0.75, meaning that inflation intensifies as budget deficits worsen. The correlation between growth in domestic credit and inflation in transitioning countries was 0.99.

The problem of inflation has been handled in the reformed countries. From 2011 to 2013, growth in the consumer price index across CEE wavered between 0% and 4% year on year, and 10 out of 12 CIS countries kept price growth to under 8% per year.

2) Labour. CEE was unable to deal with the problem of unemployment during the development stage, and the problem only intensified once a number of countries joined the EU. For example, unemployment reached 19.5% of the workforce in Lithuania (2010), 18.9% in Slovakia (2000), 17.9% in Poland (2005), 17.8% in Latvia (2010), 17.2% in Croatia (2013), 16.7% in Estonia (2010), and 16.4% in Bulgaria (2000). Unemployment also led to labour migration out of Albania, Lithuania, Romania, the Czech Republic, and other countries.

The CIS did not generally have an unemployment problem, though higher labour expenditures pushed inflation higher. A lack of unemployment in some CIS countries can be explained by faulty statistical accounting (a slow transition to the methodology employed by the International Labour Organization), and in others by hidden unemployment (part-time work, temporary leaves of absence initiated by employers, and more), though several did, in fact, have unemployment (2009 saw unemployment of 16.9% in Georgia) as well as labour migration abroad.

3) Capital. Yearly growth in foreign direct investment in the CIS during the development stage amounted to about 30%; in CEE that number was 25%. However, the share attracted by those countries continued to be insignificant: in 1993 the CIS brought in 0.77% of global foreign direct investment, by 2000 it had dropped to 0.19%, and by 2012 it had rebounded to 2.34%. The CEE's numbers for 1993, 2000, and 2012 were 2.57%, 2.58%, and 2.59%, respectively.

The primary driver for growth in the flow of investment directed toward CEE was privatization; the CIS pushed ahead thanks to growth in prices for energy resources that brought foreign investors into the oil and gas industry (60% of all foreign direct investment in CIS countries was gobbled up by Russia, Kazakhstan, and Azerbaijan).

Countries began to borrow heavily in search of financing. While foreign debt was not generally a problem, the debt taken out by a number of countries exceeded their GDP: 167.4% of GDP in Serbia (2000), 133.6% in Moldova (2000), and 131.8% in Kyrgyzstan (1999).

Continual stimuli and self-discipline are essential to long-haul reforms during the development period. CEE countries wanted to join the EU, which incentivized them, unlike those in the CIS, to actively pursue reform. Moreover, almost all CEE countries (with the exception of Latvia) accelerated reforms before joining the EU and relaxed them immediately afterwards, with most even reversing over time (see Table 8).

So it looks as though the EU was the main incentive for CEE countries to implement reforms and finish transition to market economy.

Table 8: Comprehensive reform index for CEE countries before and after joining the EU[85,86,87,88,89]

Country (year of entry)	Index value (year before joining the EU)	Index value (year after joining the EU)	Index value in 2013
Poland (2004)	3.55 (2003)	3.66 (2005)	3.66
Slovenia (2004)	3.55 (2003)	3.33 (2005)	3.16
Hungary (2004)	3.77 (2003)	3.88 (2005)	3.38
Slovakia (2004)	3.33 (2003)	3.66 (2005)	3.38
Latvia (2004)	3.55 (2003)	3.55 (2005)	3.61
Estonia (2004)	3.33 (2003)	3.66 (2005)	3.61
Lithuania (2004)	3.55 (2003)	3.55 (2005)	3.33
Bulgaria (2007)	3.55 (2006)	3.55 (2008)	3.22
Romania (2007)	2.88 (2006)	3.44 (2008)	3.33
Croatia (2013)	3.33 (2012)	3.22 (2013)	3.22

After becoming the EU members CEE countries were continuing fighting with the 'middle-income' pitfall. Those who kept on reforming, for example, Poland, Lithuania, Latvia, Estonia, Hungary, Slovakia and the Czech Republic, managed to leave this trap. This demonstrates that the speed of reforms is more important than the level of development when a country starts reforming. As an example, in the 1990s, some CEE countries, like Poland, Hungary, Slovakia, and the Czech Republic were on a similar level of development with other emerging economies, like Mexico, Malaysia, Thailand, and Turkey. But the CEE countries managed to overcome the 'middle-income' pitfall, and the latter couldn't do that.[90]

Unlike CEE, the CIS has other incentives for further structural reform: slowing national and regional economies, Russia's growing geopolitical influence, nation-building ideology, populism, conservatism aimed at preserving political power, China's economic expansion, the recommendations of international organizations, and more.

China went through an economic transformation similar to that of CEE and the CIS, remaking itself into a superpower and building a new economic normalcy over the course of several decades.

CHAPTER 4

THE CHINESE EXPERIENCE

China usually stands alone as a unique case of reform. A monolith of a country with a long history spanning changes in both leadership and economic fortunes, it has held onto its language, culture, cuisine, and genetics, while coming up with a litany of inventions along the way. For millennia China was the world's only economic and political superpower, though its economic and cultural peak was the Tang dynasty (618–906), and the Silk Road it left behind. The compass, paper, paper money, gunpowder, porcelain, and printing, were all invented in China. At the beginning of the 15th century, Zheng He explored the Indian Ocean, drawing maps that would later be used by Columbus and Magellan. However, China's reorientation toward internal sources of development isolated it from the outside world. The Industrial Revolution which England experienced in the 19th century was not felt in China, serving only to drive it deeper into an economic depression that ended with the fall of the Qing dynasty's three centuries of rule in 1911. Stunningly, in 1820, during its deep economic depression, China still created more than 30% of the world's GDP (by way of comparison, in 2019 the US made up only around 25% of it). Mao Zedong's Great Leap Forward and the Cultural Revolution were unable to return the country to the path of historical revival; it was only Deng Xiaoping's economic reform that unlocked energy, growth, development, and forward momentum, toward the national dream.

A policy of economic reform and openness

Deng Xiaoping's reforms, an opening demographic window of opportunity, and a number of other factors, including strict adherence to an economic strategy, allowed China to transform itself economically while leaving political stability intact.

1.1 The formation of an economic ideology

The first step China took toward transformation occurred from 1978 to 1984. It began with agriculture, which moved *en masse* to a family contract system. The communal production system in place was replaced by a new system of individual responsibility. State and collective property began to enjoy more equal rights. A new dual-use system was implemented for land: communes went beyond state use to offer the land to individual farmers on a long-term rental basis. Economic associations were formed in agriculture that combined the financial weight of villages, towns, and small cities in an effort to boost the wellbeing of entire regions. All of that was fairly transparent, which inspired trust on the part of the rural villagers themselves, and the reforms enjoyed popular support for the most part. The economic success of one province pushed others to carry out their own reforms while also pushing the central government to go still further.

Communist China saw the rise of a new socio-economic model based on the pursuit of profit. Social and ecological standards, social inequality, and informal connections were given limited room to grow. A new pluralism of ideas appeared in the economy, widening the search for new solutions. Concentration on personal wellbeing as opposed to political freedom made it possible to blow off political steam, preserve social stability, solve the problem of national self-identity, and leave behind the point of no return to the communism of Marx and Mao. Interestingly, in 2001 that ideology was made official by the Communist Party of China in its Three Represents doctrine, according to which the party is required to represent the interests of business as well as those of the working class and peasants. Even in the era of Xi Jingpin, reform-rhetoric continues to be the symbol of pragmatism and common sense in China.

1.2 Reforming state ownership

The priorities during the second step (1984–1992) were oriented toward setting up a favorable business climate and transforming ownership forms, which changed their proportions. By 1992 the share of GDP created by state enterprises had dropped to 40%; 50% was taken by collective forms of ownership and the rest went to privately owned and mixed forms.[91]

In 1995, China began privatizing small state-owned enterprises while holding onto the larger ones. First, the 1000 largest were held back and the small and medium-sized were privatized or forced into insolvency. Over the next five years another 435 of those 1000 major state-owned companies also went through bankruptcy proceedings. A number of ministries dependent on those enterprises were reformed as holdings and subjected to a new corporate management system. Ultimately, they were designated as critical or non-critical, with the non-critical companies restructured and privatized.

As a result of these reforms, China currently has around 100 central state-owned enterprises that report to the State-Owned Assets Supervision and Administration Commission of the State Council, and create around 30% of GDP. The rest are private businesses, mostly small and medium-sized, which create more than 70% of GDP, pay 80% of taxes, and account for 90% of jobs. The private sector in China is primarily driven by small and medium business, which creates 60% of GDP as well as 60% of the country's exports.[92] China's state-owned enterprises cover strategic industries like petrochemicals, gas, coal, energy, non-ferrous metallurgy, space, and more.

1.3 Reforming the company management system

The incentive mechanism for the directors of Chinese state-owned enterprises developed in lockstep with the surrounding economic environment. To start off with, from 1987 to the middle of the 1990s, China featured a contractual responsibility system. Directors signed contracts that laid out goals to be achieved by their companies: yearly profit transferred to the state coffers, production levels, proceeds denominated in foreign currency, taxes, loss reduction, debt reduction, and more. They could also receive a fixed percentage of their companies' earnings and tax receipts in addition to their base salary. In an attempt to incentivize directors to exceed the goals set for them, they also enjoyed a system whereby they received progressively larger percentages of the profit that stayed in their companies. Contracts for the first time included year-end bonuses, which stood at around 20% of their base salary at the beginning of the 1990s, and the contractual responsibility system also saw the introduction of contractually obligated golden parachutes in case directors of state-owned enterprises were released before their contracts expired.

Directors of major Chinese state-owned enterprises currently receive a fixed salary (around USD 5,000-6,000 a month), a yearly bonus (a percentage of revenue that can exceed base salary), and a percentage of total contract amounts (from 0.5% to 5% in a one-time payment made once the contract is signed). They also have a social package that includes housing, healthcare, vacation time, and education for them and their families. Interestingly, directors of state-owned joint-stock companies also have a put option that lets them buy shares in their own companies at a cheap, nominal price and sell them on the financial market at the market price whenever they want. As growth in stock prices in China accelerated through 2006–2008, those options began to play the lead role when it came to incentivizing directors. *Caijing*, a Chinese financial magazine, published information in 2008 showing that the difference between the price of stock in China's Mobile, a state-owned company, for the company's management and their current market price was USD 9 billion.

One more critical factor driving the success of directors of Chinese state-owned companies is their almost complete independence. Astonishingly, neither tax nor law-enforcement, nor any other state agencies, get involved in the business of state enterprises. Tax audits are only held when tax laws are broken, something that usually happens once every three to five years. Directors usually sign three-year contracts and are evaluated along with their companies at the end of those contracts. During those three years, however, they are free to handle all business decisions, including the amount of contracts they sign.

In 2016-2019, within 'supply-side' structural reform, China widely introduced the system of corporate management at its state-owned enterprises, decreasing the levels of management from 5-7 to 3-5.

1.4 Liberalizing prices and creating a financial market

China brought in two Nobel laureates, Joseph Stiglitz and Kenneth Arrow, to offer scientific support for the reforms the government was running, and the two scientists' first recommendation was to liberalize prices and create institutional infrastructure in the form of a financial market. Prices were set by the market, though the shift was initially only partial: a dual system was put in place whereby companies were required to meet the previously set quotas and sell those goods at fixed prices. Everything they produced after having met those quotas could be sold at market prices. Then, in 1992, the State Council of the People's Republic of China gave state-owned enterprises full control over their prices and salaries. Beginning in the 1990s, prices on almost all products (with the exception of some raw materials like coal, oil, and gas) were set by the market.

A financial market was created in China, thanks to the local initiatives of Shanghai and Shenzhen. In December 1990, a currency and stock exchange opened in Shanghai, and by 1992, 30 companies were listed. By 1997, that number had grown to 383. The second largest Chinese exchange opened in Shenzhen in July 1991. In 1992, 24 companies were listed, and five years later there were already 362.[93] From 1993 to 2010, Chinese state-owned companies alone brought in 651 billion dollars from the financial market, comparable to the total amount of foreign investments made in China over the same period. A limited liberalization of the financial market boosted its attractiveness and led to booms in 2007 and 2015, especially for high-tech companies. With that said, the stock market in China is undercapitalized. In 1991 it was valued at around 40% of GDP, in 2007 at 178%, in 2015 at around 90%, and in 2018-2019 it went down to 50-70%. Developed countries generally stay above 100% of GDP.

It is important to note that Chinese companies prefer their initial public offering to be abroad, for example, in Hong Kong or New York. Listing in international markets lets them attract well-known investment bankers whose names alone are enough to guarantee the quality of the stocks being offered. Chinese stocks are also issued partially (20–30% of the total), which limits the supply and inflates their price. With that said, demand for stocks often reflects international investors' attitudes toward China itself, rather than towards the Chinese issuers themselves. Once stocks are issued on international exchanges they are then issued in China, with Chinese investors informed by the international quotation.

1.5 Bringing in FDI

Foreign direct investments were attracted to China by tax breaks, special economic zones, the size of the market, and low production costs (labour costs in particular, considering the rural-to-urban migration). In 2001, China joined the WTO, which also served as a signal for investors and enlivened a stream of foreign direct investment that grew more than a hundred times over 30 years.

Hong Kong is the main investor in China, followed by the Virgin Islands, Japan, and South Korea. One peculiarity of foreign investment attracted to China is that around a third of all foreign investors in the country are ethnic Chinese. They own many transnational corporations in

Southeast Asia. At least 12 Chinese families are worth more than 5 billion dollars each, and 16 of the 200 richest people in the world belong to the Chinese diaspora. They generally invest in regions from which their ancestors emigrated, and so the Chinese authorities have created special economic zones incorporating those areas that offer free land and infrastructure, guarantee capital, and include high positions in the government.

The second third of foreign investors in China is made up of Chinese companies manufacturing abroad and returning to China in search of tax breaks. The breaks they are offered are seen by many experts as long-term tax amnesties offered to bring capital back into the country. *The Financial Times* estimates that the capital illegally smuggled out of China in the 1980s and 1990s amounted to 100 billion dollars, and the preferential income tax rates offered to foreign investors from 1994 to 2007 also incentivized the return of Chinese investment. The fixed preferential tax system that was in place saw foreign direct investment grow by a factor of 1.8, to 67.3 billion dollars in 2007.

The final third of investors is made up of major transnational corporations investing in a technology-for-market exchange. Initially joint companies were popular: transnationals brought the money and technology while their Chinese counterparts contributed the land and buildings. Today more than 80% of foreign companies are completely foreign, which is explained by the growth of local technology as well as national educational and innovation programs in China.

On January 1 2020, the new law on foreign investments was introduced in China. Previously closed industries were opened for foreign companies to boost FDI inflow and competition.

1.6 Stimulating exports

Chinese exports were initially built on imitating innovation and supported by tax breaks, a partial VAT return, soft loans for exporters and their buyers, a favorable currency policy, and low labour and other production costs. That gave Chinese exporters up to a 40% price advantage (China has been the world's largest exporter since 2009) and led to strong growth in the current account surplus.

Tech imports were cultivated in an effort to boost quality and cope with new competitors (their share of total imports in the 2000s was around 60%). On average, approximately two thirds of the value of high-tech exports coming out of China were created abroad. That number was even higher for exported laptops, displays, cellphones, DVD players, and CD players, for which almost the entire value of the end product was created outside China. Recently the growth of domestic technology has pushed the share of imports in exports down to 35%. As a result, the 'Made in China' model went from 'Assembled in China' to 'Created in China'. The national programs 'Made in China 2025', and 'Internet+' provide indicators and state policy for high-tech development in the country and the import of innovative products to China.

1.7 Chinese direct investment: staying in and going out

From 2000 to 2014 Chinese direct investment abroad grew from 1 to 120 billion dollars. Chinese investment in other countries is aimed at supporting exports and unlocking access to resources, innovation, and brands. Most money (around 70% of all investments) is invested in nearby Asian countries, followed by Latin America (15%), Europe (8%), and North America (4%). More than 90% of all Chinese direct investment in the Eurasian Economic Community is taken up by Kazakhstan. On the whole, China pursues a highly pragmatic policy when it comes to foreign markets for goods and capital in keeping with the idea that soft power means making a profit without asking the wrong political questions.

Since 2008, under the shadow cast by the global crisis, the Chinese government has actively invested in infrastructure and real estate in order to stimulate domestic sources of growth. That changed 'Made in China' to 'Made for China' and inflated the domestic market. Government investment accounted for a fifth of economic growth, accelerated urbanization, and, thanks to low mortgage rates, made real estate an attractive asset for the Chinese (on a par with the financial market). That was accompanied by growth in investment and consumer demand, and an uptick in real estate prices, and administrative limits placed on obtaining property, thanks to which ghost cities full of unoccupied and newly constructed buildings began to appear. Obsolescence and depreciation now overtake projects before they can even be developed.

When all is said, the transformation of the Chinese economy boosted the country's status. The political heft China wields today is symbolized by its GDP (second largest in the world after the US), its strong yearly growth rate (9.5% in 1978–1992, 9.8% in 1993–2002, 11.7% in 2003–2012, 6.9% in 2013-2019), its world's largest currency stockpile (around 3.4 trillion dollars), and the capitalization of Chinese corporations and banks. China's share of global GDP rose from 12.6% to 14.7% just from 2009 to 2012 and to 16.2% in 2019.

Most importantly, however, living standards grew, and continue to grow. GDP per capita based on purchasing power parity rose from 302 dollars in 1978 to 10,900 dollars in 2012 and 15,376 dollars in 2018, and the average salary went from 10 dollars in 1978 to 554 dollars in 2012, and more than 900 dollars in 2019. Moreover, China saw the appearance of a middle class, complete with new challenges and demands for further growth in the country's socio-economic model. Nowadays the Chinese middle class covers 30% of the population - or 400 million Chinese.

New economic normality

Xi Jinping brought a new stage of development to China when he came to power in 2012. In contrast to Hu Jintao, the preceding General Secretary of the Communist Party of China, who pursued measured, scientifically informed governance (political decisions were made based on analysis of the problems they were designed to solve). Xi Jinping was immediately more active, favoring action over words and pragmatism without demagoguery. The government he appointed, with Li Keqiang at its head, positioned itself as a group of reformers moving away from microeconomics to focus on the country's overall development strategy. The ideological rhetoric changed as well: socialism with a Chinese flavor, or the idea of reviving the nation and uniting it around the common goal of its prosperity, became the Chinese dream.

Along with that, in 2011–2014, for the first time in the past few decades, China's growth slowed and the new reference point became 7.5%. That intensified the discussion taking place over replacing GDP as the primary economic objective. Shanghai pioneered this movement by excluding GDP growth from its regional goals for the first time in 2015, replacing it with metrics measuring quality of life, pollution, innovation, and development of green and blue (water) economies. Reducing GDP growth rates and switching the focus to productivity and quality earned the moniker of a new economic normality, with the following features:[94][95]

2.1 Changing the economic structure

A) Growth in the service sector. The Chinese economy slowed due to an internal reorganization: in 2013 the service sector outpaced the manufacturing and construction industries for the first time, creating 46%

as opposed to 44% of GDP. In 2018, the service sector took more than half of the economy – 58% of GDP. Employment in manufacturing had already levelled off at the end of the 1990s, and urbanization brought a new demand for the urban services that accompany it. The IT sector is also growing, while education and healthcare are becoming more commercialized. Given the fact that labour productivity is generally lower in the service sector than in manufacturing as it is, this holds back total output.

B) Growth in domestic consumption and slowing exports. From 2010 to 2018, consumption's share of GDP went from 48% to 76%, while that of net exports fell from 7% to 2%. Higher wages and highly flexible exchange rates curtailed Chinese exports and pushed imports higher. Export-heavy industries began to contract due to reduced internal migration and an aging population. Even the structure of domestic consumption changed: a new focus on quality, global brands, and ecological and social standards appeared. A novel behavioral model of avoiding work, and living on savings while investing in finance and real estate instead, emerged.

2.2 Exporting capital instead of goods

A) A new Silk Road. China continued to invest abroad in an effort to support its construction companies, contractors, and export industries experiencing overproduction. The year 2013 saw the appearance of 'One Belt, One Road', a new Silk Road project aimed at creating a 'belt' of economic growth. Part of a strategy designed to support construction outside China, the project's primary goals are to create infrastructural, financial, and telecommunication interdependency between the participating countries in addition to removing reciprocal trade barriers. A fund worth 40 billion dollars was created to support the project, though experts say most of the money will not be spent on the Eurasian part of the plan; instead, it will go toward securing China's position on the sea route, something that concerns the US and its interests in Asia.

B) New ways for Chinese to invest abroad. Interestingly, about 40% of Chinese investment abroad is in private companies, something that may speak to a capital drain flowing out of the country. Investment targets are also changing: China started investing more in the financial sector (in the interests of expanding international operations using the RMB in Europe), in non-traditional industries (the postal service in Singapore and media outlets in South Korea), and more. In its turn, the

Chinese government worried that Chinese companies invested in the countries 'with no order', with the risk of civil war, or in projects with little rate of return, like entertainment, hotels, and sport. So in 2017, Chinese government created a 'negative list' of industries, and restricted the industries where Chinese companies could invest abroad.

2.3 Debt overhang

Significant government investment, especially in municipal bonds, after 2008 intensified the government's debt problem. That problem has also been complicated by the frequent indistinguishability of finances at state-owned companies, state banks, and local governments; the development of shadow banking (for example, in Wenzhou) and how it has intertwined itself with official banking; distorted lending to state-owned companies by state banks; problems assessing and assigning securities; bringing in short-term loans for long-term projects; and more. As a result, the totality of debt held by the Chinese government is 300% of GDP according to the highest estimates. With that said, that level of debt can be stomached when considering that the lion's share is domestic debt, meaning that both the creditors and the borrowers report to the government. The authorities also allowed defaults to go through in several companies in order to enforce financial discipline.

2.4 Fighting corruption

Different estimations claim that bribes and embezzlement in China amounted to 4–5% of the country's GDP during the 2000s. Taking a bribe worth more than 13,500 dollars is punishable by over ten years in prison or the death penalty, and around 20,000 people are punished for corruption every year. On the other hand, experts say that no more than 6% of the officials who are caught taking bribes are punished.

Xi Jinping brought new vigor to the fight against corruption, something that was once seen almost as a driver of economic growth. Wang Qishan, Secretary of the Central Commission for Discipline Inspection (now vice-Chairman of China), organized the fight against corruption into three stages: gradually cleansing personnel, strengthening the rule of law, and installing a new generation of officials. Once a new agency was formed as part of the first stage from 2011 to 2014 the number of highly placed officials investigated rose from 200 to 600 (see Illustration 3). In total, in 2014, 270 thousand officials of different levels were arrested. In 2015, this was 330 thousand, in 2016 – 415 thousand, in 2017 – 527 thousand, in 2018 – 621 thousand, and in 2019 – 587 thousand.[96][97] The scale of banquets as well as the value and number of gifts also dropped. This sometimes leads to important decisions being put off, out of fear of making a mistake, connections between competitors being cultivated in order to keep an agency from digging up old skeletons, and the government being left with unfilled vacancies. Moreover, an anticorruption campaign led to money outflow from the country. Since 2014, billions of dollars have been flying out of China, although before that, it was millions. In 2015, 674 billion dollars left China, and in 2016, it was 725 billion dollars.[98]

Illustration 3. The number of highly placed officials investigated, 1991–2014[99]

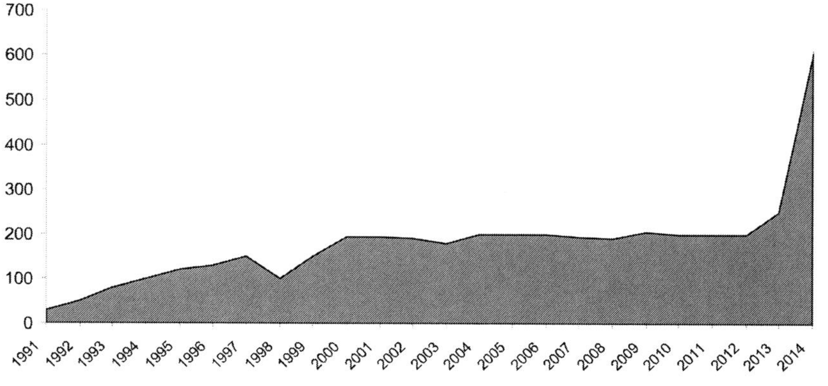

Not satisfied with hunting for corrupt officials within the country, China declared war on former offenders who fled overseas (an operation codenamed Skynet). Requests to hand over suspects were sent to the US specifically.

2.5 Structural economic reforms

Li Keqiang's government considers its mission to be continuing structural reforms aimed at developing the country's market economy. The primary elements of reform are: changing the priorities for government investment; making life easier for the business sector; and fiscally supporting small and medium businesses, for example, via the income tax and capital requirements for banks financing small businesses.

Finance has been liberalized, though that has, so far, extended only to the loan rates that the state regulates, while leaving deposit rates alone. Control over tax breaks has been toughened. Budgetary constraints have eased when it comes to bailing out local authorities, state banks, and state-owned companies (the monetary base grew from 19% in 2008 to 29% in 2009 during a period of active government investment). A new emphasis has been placed on developing public-private partnerships, including by expanding areas where the economy regulates itself. In 2015, a 2020 plan was announced that will include restructuring 'zombie companies' (unproductive state-owned corporations draining financial resources from the healthy economy) by declaring which are profitable, and bringing in private investment or beginning bankruptcy proceedings. Social spending is also increasing: in 2009 a ten-year plan was announced that will devote 120 billion dollars to expanding the country's healthcare system, such that it will eventually cover every last village and every last citizen.

The Chinese experience of economic reform may look different when compared to those implemented in CEE and CIS countries over the same period of time. That impression, however, is due solely to the sheer size of the Chinese economy and its global effect. In reality, the reforms and their consequences are both similar and recognizable, leading to the conclusion that there are common rules, mechanisms and general manual for economic transformation.

Part 3.

The Manual for Economic Reforms

CHAPTER 5

ECONOMIC TRANSFORMATION: RULES AND MECHANISMS

Some ground rules and mechanisms for transformation need to be established before beginning specific economic reforms aimed at liberalization, creating a competitive market, building institutions, and so on. They are the logic of economic transformation. Losing any link in the chain could slow, or even reverse, the progress of reform.

The process by which economic reform takes place is anything but chaos; it follows a strict order. And it is not simply putting out the fires of internal and external drivers necessitating change. Instead, there are strict internal rules and mechanisms that have been developed based on the rich practical experience built up by a variety of economic entities: individuals,[100] small and medium businesses,[101] big enterprises,[102][103] and countries at different levels of development.[104][105][106]

The rules for economic transformation

Every rule answers a simple question: why, where to, what, how, when, who, and for whom?

Rule 1: priorities determine the strategy

1) Why?

Before jumping into economic reforms it is important to understand why they are needed in the first place and figure out what is holding the economy back—which entities, industries, decisions, laws, or controlling agencies. It is critical to both understand and acknowledge whether existing priorities are capable of getting the most out of the economy and whether they can drive stable growth, support economic development, and insulate from internal and external shocks. If those priorities are unclear, they can be discerned by analyzing the resources spent on them; finances, time, labour, and other.

Recognizing the need for different priorities and new ideas to put at the heart of the overall economic strategy is the first step, and a first condition for reform. Without that, all subsequent steps taken will be artificial, and the people in charge of development and execution will, themselves, not believe in them. With that said, the question of why reform is needed cannot morph into a search for who is to blame. Finger-pointing detracts from the issue at hand and sacrifices the professionals needed to implement reform.

The Nobel Laureate in Economics, Jean Tirole, in his book *Economics for the Common Good,* outlines a few principles for state reform:[107]

1. Use benchmarks to convince. Compare with the best international practices and understand the reasons for the differences;
2. Identify the best way to address the problem. If the private sector can do it better, why not try it that way?;
3. Do not cut across the board. Identify what's essential as well as what is not, what works, as well as what doesn't;
4. Monitor the conformity of policies with objectives.

2) Where to?

The necessity of change leads to the selection of a new strategic goal for long-term development. That could be GDP per capita, living standards, labour productivity, or something else. However, in view of today's growing openness and mobility, countries can no longer focus on simply improving their position year on year; they have to outpace the rest of the pack. In other words, countries, just like people and companies, face competition, and so chasing down a specific competitor becomes the new strategic goal.

The aim for the new priorities driving the strategy, therefore, is development focused on outstripping the competition. The government could set its sights on nearby countries with similar geographical and cultural contexts, or simply any other similarly sized country with comparable potential.

3) What?

Priorities can be set as steps to achieve the strategic goal once it has been established, and those priorities are grounded in limited resources. After all, it is easier to hit a home run and jump to the front of the pack in just one or a couple of key areas than in many, or even all, of them. That requires pushing concentrated resources (raw materials, finances, technology, human capital, time) in specific directions. The opposite approach, that of developing on all fronts simultaneously, would also end up prioritized due to limited resources, though that would only happen once those resources have been thoroughly scattered. Another option—spreading resources between industries—would distort them all, driving unstable development and engendering uncertainty in how to move forward economically and socially. Priorities therefore push past lobbying and help avoid contradictions in decision-making. It is also important to note that concentrating resources to support a small number of priorities helps create an economy of scale, letting small countries specialize in specific products and compete on an equal footing with their larger counterparts.

Priorities should be reviewed, confirmed, and modified regularly. It is simply impossible to account for everything—unpredictable ecological catastrophes, world wars and crises, oscillating oil prices, currency exchange rates, et al. Laying out long-term priorities is like keeping a fire brigade ready: you never know where or when there will be a fire, so you put together and constantly train an energetic and effective team capable of reacting to both normal and unforeseen situations.[108]

4) How?

This stage needs a new idea to inspire the more active segment of society (the middle class, scientists, the machinery of state, entrepreneurs) and unite it as a whole. Having like-minded and creative people is important when it comes to developing reforms, but carrying them out requires a new economic shove: social energy as well as moral and psychological motivation fixed on strategic positivity and inspiration.

The government can call on a number of different types of social ideas as part of its economic transformation:

A) Collective liberalism, which is not a pluralism of varying opinions and movements; rather, it is a common focus on solving a concrete economic problem.[109] The unifying goal can be, for example, the country's economic development and boosting prosperity by jointly implementing liberal economic tools and mechanisms for public control and supervision.

B) A socialized economy geared towards providing social guarantees for every individual (food security, a job, a fair wage, a pension, and so on) and meeting public needs (promoting education, science, and culture). A socialized economy differs from state capitalism in that public needs are met exclusively by utilizing market relationships: private property, unfettered competition, and more. The main way this mechanism can be employed is via tax policy. A similar approach referred to as 'new pragmatism' is currently making the rounds of Polish and Russian economists.[110][111]

C) A positive economy, at the heart of which is altruistic selfishness as a model for business and behavior. Its essence is that "…all businessmen want to sell their products. If people are happy with them, they will buy them. And for people to be happy with them, the seller needs to first step into their shoes".[112] That approach works for more than just business; it is also for individuals, the government, and society, calling everyone on all levels to keep long-term strategic development in mind, let that instruct collective interaction, and build a positive system of KPIs.

Answers to the questions of why reforms are needed, where they are heading, what the new priorities will be, and which ideas unite society and lie at the heart of change make it possible to put together a new strategy for economic development. That strategy is the first step down the road to economic transformation.

Rule 2: The strategy determines the structure

1) Why?

The question of why the structure should be changed comes up if priorities have already been altered and a new strategy has already been laid out. The answer is that the existing economic structure always reflects someone's old interests, and they will conflict with the new priorities and the newly developed strategy. With that in mind, the new economic structure is built on those new priorities and that new strategy. Discipline is critical, as the new strategy can only be approved and followed in the understanding that the old ways and methods are also the reasons why reform is needed in the first place.

When it comes to figuring out why a new structure is needed, we can just look at this analogy: for a bus to be turned into a plane (an airbus), it will only fly once the decision has been made, a plan has been developed, and its structure has been reworked. Structural reforms lie at the core of economic transformation.

2) How?

Structural economic reform (of industries, property, or regulation) has been driven around the world by a number of factors. Most often these have been technological revolutions and/or economic crises. The ascent of a tech industry leads to cyclical restructuring: new goods create and strengthen demand, and new technology lowers expenses and prices. That, in turn, still further stimulates demand, and lays the groundwork for overproduction, until those new products melt into the old and innovation repeats itself. A perfect example in the 19th century was the implementation of the steam engine and railroad construction, which injected new life into the coal industry. In the 20th century, heavy engineering, electric energy, automobile construction, and oil refining, all had their day in the sun. At the beginning of this century it was the turn of the internet, telecommunications, and robotics.

The boom in labour productivity after the advent of the internet turned out to be much shorter than the growth experienced after the internal combustion engine was invented. That renewed the discussion in scientific circles about the depletion of innovation and a long-term deceleration for the global economy.[113] At the same time, claims pointing to a complete halt in technological progress and structural economic transformation are dubious. Even today, it is clearer than ever that the coming decades will see the economy change under the influence of alternative energy, information overload, and the implementation of information processing technology. The global economy will most likely also change, due to goods, capital, people, and information, that can cross borders with ease; the urbanization of developing countries; the debt problems developed countries are experiencing; aging populations; and other factors.

3) When?

Transformation is better implemented in periods of stability, rather than waiting for crises and the necessity they bring with them. Stability is when the economy has the reserves it needs to create a security mechanism and quietly carry out reforms, perform experiments, and try out new methods and tools. Unfortunately, that rarely happens, given the fact that decision-makers are usually the last to learn when reforms are needed.[114] First, are generally the middle and local managers who are in constant contact with the outside world. By the time information and recognition of the inevitability of reform reaches the people in charge of the economy, time has passed and the situation has become critical. And yet the great majority of the reforms, for example in Sweden, Finland, Germany, and Canada, were made precisely under difficult conditions. So, there are cases when a difficult economic situation can help, not hinder, reforms.[115]

Immediate and complete reform sometimes paralyzes the entire economic management system. On the one hand, pursuing it too quickly leaves precious little time to adapt, compounding old problems with new ones and greasing the wheels for mistakes to be made. On the other hand, going too slowly leads to problems building up and quietly festering until they explode with all the more intensity, demanding even faster and more decisive measures.

The initial stage of structural reform as part of a new strategy is when the rubber meets the road. It is a time of doubt, contradiction, and acting under external influence (changes in technology, crises, and more). Unfortunately, going from the first rule to the second rarely happens when it should, and often leads to the third rule.

Rule 3: The structure determines the personnel

1) Who?

While old personnel have a hard time adapting quickly to a new structure, new personnel cannot implement fresh ideas in an old structure. And for that reason the right people have to be brought in for new priorities, strategies, and structures. The best option is a symbiosis of like-minded thinkers made up of both old and new, though the newcomers have to come from outside the system and politics in order to avoid lobbying by narrow, departmental interests and a dependence on popular opinion.

The managers currently in place need to have a desire for reform, an open discussion, and self-discipline in order for that reform to happen. However, that is complicated and sometimes conflict-ridden when new hires are made, new consultants are brought in, and reformers take the spotlight. The new faces have to be ready to risk their reputation and relationships with current management, by speaking sometimes unpleasant truths to powerful people. Often, they feel their way around, isolated and under threat of being fired at any moment.[116] It is critical that they be competent in order to avoid subverting the entire idea of reform, while there is a critical mass of those willing to run with their suggestions that must be achieved. Newcomers have to complement, rather than replace existing managers, otherwise crisis and paralysis will infect the entire management structure. Of course, sometimes old managers do need to be forced out in order to avoid repeating old mistakes.

2) For whom?

Reforms are best carried out when most people see their value throughout the entire process. It is harder to evaluate the costs: were they brought on by the reforms or were they there necessitating the reforms all along? It is also important to differentiate between short-term and long-term costs and benefits.

The benefits of structural economic reform in the short term are an influx of foreign direct investment and the creation of new, highly productive jobs. In the long run they are steady, measured economic growth, lowered inflation, and a standard of living that draws progressively to that of developed countries.

The costs in the short term are falling real GDP, production, and consumption; higher unemployment; labour migration out of the country; inflation; and falling standards of living. In the long run, they are chronically higher unemployment and some oscillation in production and consumption levels.

Obviously, structural economic reform is unpopular—the short-term headache weighs heavier on society than the short- and long-term benefits. A desire to put off reform can therefore grow into the temptation to continue making promises without ever letting off the brakes or even getting started in the first place. Ultimately, that is the critical phenomenon of structural reform: reformers only earn trust if their reforms are actually unpopular and they still follow through with them. At that point international organizations, creditors, and investors get on the bandwagon and the dam breaks, letting the river of loans and direct investment rush in. There is no other way to make economic transformation more palatable for society—economic development without structural reform is unstable and still does not usually lead to long-term social stability. It is important to understand the cost of structural economic reforms: lowered present standards of living sacrificed in the interest of strong future growth.

Economic transformation leaves no one untouched, though the true costs are saved for those who are least flexible and least adaptable. While change can be delayed by heavy opposition, the necessity of progress eventually wins the day and leads to a change in personnel. If the reforms are well explained and made early enough, they are often rewarded by the electorate.

Once the rule-based logic of economic transformation has been mastered, the next important step is to choose the right mechanism for economic reform by understanding the measures that need to be taken.

Mechanisms for economic transformation

The available mechanisms for economic reform can be categorized by the degree of state intervention in the economy they entail. There are three options for how that transformation looks in practice:

1) Holding onto the old economic structure;
2) Manually altering the economic structure by constant management of, and control over, the process;
3) Fostering a free economic structure.

It is important to note that those mechanisms can be alternatives to each other in the short term when looking for ways to minimize the costs borne by society. In the long term, they are a three-step plan that moves from the first option to the second, and finishes with the third. With that in mind, the decision is less a choice between mechanisms and more a selection of the speed at which they will transition from one to another. The economy itself gives the green light for when that transition should happen via its metrics, how fast it is growing and developing, and society's living standards.

The first mechanism: holding onto the old economic structure

In this case the economy develops by business as usual, or through the inertial force built up by what has already been achieved. Slowed economic growth, a financial deficit, and a worsening situation can highlight the features of this mechanism at the macro and micro levels. Regardless, priorities, strategies, and structures remain unchanged; further growth and development is engineered by personnel changes.

1. The macro level

Priorities and tools for economic policy are set at the macro level on a reactionary basis depending on the problems that arise. The monetary side is preoccupied by chronically high inflation or periodic deflation; priorities change when more pressing societal concerns pop up, for example, unemployment or the importance of boosting income to the level of neighboring countries. As a result, many decisions are made with an eye towards preserving the current economic structure. 'Don't fix it if it ain't broken', 'better to rename than to replace', and 'kicking the can down the road', are the name of the game. Economic problems are explained away as due to external factors or short-/long-term dips in the global economy. At the same time, the situation improves for competitors, meaning that growth in the share of domestic products on the market begins to slow, or even decline.

Macroeconomists move away from their professional development, or are continually reforming in order to catch up to, and surpass, competitors, as well as pushing economic growth, in favor of optimistically just doing their duty and limiting their planning to the short term. Short-term results tumbling in one after another become the strategy. The criteria for success are how fast and frequently results are achieved, instead of steady progress and stability. Actions have to be taken faster and faster in order to maintain economic growth. Subtle financial and statistical manipulation is used to achieve goals, and is therefore considered a valid and useful tool. Sadly, that kind of manipulation generally utilizes stress, force, and fear, at the cost of inspiration and initiative.

In the end, a wobbling foundation of random results is jerry-rigged in place of the solid foundation of trust the macroeconomy needs. Long-term prospects for macroeconomic development are built on hopes and even plans for an unknown stroke of luck that will put everything right in the economy.

2. The micro level

Manual management maintains, and even expands, its position at the micro level. At the same time, however, problems in the microeconomy build up and begin to characterize more and more companies, and even industries. Micro-problems become widespread and systemic, even wielding a macroeconomic effect. More complex, non-standard, and unpopular (structural) solutions become needed, though they are considered extreme within this mechanism, and kept for when the problems are made clear and obvious to the point that the solution presents itself.

The problems building up in the microeconomy are handled the way they always have been. Decisions in quickly worsening situations are either put off or made quickly and superficially, though deficits in financial or other resources see them limited by the enforcement of the external status quo and higher labour discipline. Fast attempts at fixing the problems of poor quality and high costs hidden in the system amount to nothing more than cracking the whip, and products themselves fall further and further behind their foreign competitors. International exhibitions and trade fairs begin to feel strange and futuristic. The attitude taken by foreign partners and competitors becomes one of reserved condescension.

If there are no positive results at the micro-level over a long period of time, responsibility for problems and decision-making is passed up from the microeconomy to the macroeconomy. Hopes for improvement in the external environment, an unexpected windfall, and yet more financial support, run rampant.

The case of Taiwan shows that the government could try to build the new structure together with the old one.[117] State-owned enterprises can operate and compete together with private companies. In that case, gradually, the stronger will survive, and it might take a longer time but seems less painful. All you have to do is to wait until the old structure fades away.

3. Waiting out the old structure

The main tool for this mechanism when other resources are limited is a periodic rotation of personnel. The newcomers do what they are told, in the context of an unaltered economic structure, clear requirements, and well-known directives. However, when there is no new strategy, those newcomers are less effective than the old guard, which was at least more experienced in supporting the old structure. They hand off the old structure and its worsening results to the next group, and the cycle continues and intensifies. High turnover also leads to continuity problems, less responsibility taken all along the chain of command, hurried work that sacrifices results, and an exodus of experienced professionals.

A lack of signals for structural change from above means that real information from below is not reported, and may even be distorted. Sometimes that is due to a fear of delivering and taking responsibility for bad news,[118] at other times it is due to feelings of indifference, apathy, and thoughtlessness.[119] Regardless, the wedge between those who are competent and those who make decisions is driven deeper. Despondency, pessimism, fatigue, and depression, begin to set in when no ways out of the situation are even being considered. Employees unwillingly follow orders that contradict their idea of what needs to happen. Even new professionals lose initiative to the administrative pressure continually exerted on their daily work. As a result, requirements are toughened and control is strengthened, inflating the influence wielded over the economy by supervisory and security agencies. Energy needed to fight off external competitors is spent in an internal struggle with limitations, rules, standards, and inspectors. And given the fact that energy itself is limited, an increased administrative presence leaves less of that energy to fight back.

This mechanism is ultimately aimed at preserving the old economic structure. Ignoring systemic problems changes the focus to hot spots, though the complexity of the system makes it impossible to guess what will cause the next chain reaction. With no plan B, simply handing down the old structure can lead to long-term stagnation and social instability. And as the economic relations become more and more complicated and modern, they get out of the traditional old structure and management of the economy. So it's harder to find a clear risk for sustainable development and even existence of the whole system. Chaos theory holds that risk is exponentially proportionate to the scale of the system, and it ends up as a house of cards in which you never know which card will bring the whole thing tumbling down. As a result, everyone stands around, waiting for the breakdown of the old structure, in order to reload the economy and begin structural reform from the ground up.

The second mechanism: manually transforming the economy

This mechanism, which intermediates between the first and the third, prioritizes the future over the current economic situation in a unique form of paternalism. In this case, politicians, bureaucrats, and scientists of which the government is comprised, consider themselves more knowledgeable and capable than what they consider to be an ill-informed society and underdeveloped market. Society, in their conception, is made up of people who live for today and for themselves, and people can even misunderstand their own interests and present a danger to each other, individually or as a whole. For that reason, the government takes on a paternalistic function and directs people who, for lack of knowledge or willpower, cannot make the most rational decisions for themselves or the people around them.

There are several forms (and combinations of forms) this mechanism can take.

1) Economic emulation

This represents a conscious prioritization of select industries on the basis of their scientific and technological outlook (generally in manufacturing). They are generalized by growing returns and are then targeted for state support. While they are getting their feet off the ground, the government provides temporary support, protection, and a monopoly with some import substitution, for example, by limiting imports of raw materials and stimulating exports of high value-added goods. Highly professional international managers are also brought in to boost those industries' competitiveness with their experience and technology. The sciences and education are generally regarded as critical to the steady socio-economic growth of the country.

History confirms the effectiveness of this mechanism. For example, the 15th–18th centuries saw the rise of Venice and Florence, followed by England and Holland, in the 19th century, it was the US and Germany, and Japan followed in the 1970s.[120] Developed countries have also been going through some reindustrialization in the 21st century. Here, however, it is important to note that that is not a return to traditional manufacturing, but is the creation of new industries spawned by robotics, nearby research facilities, and major markets; the foundation of consumer demand. The economic stimulus for growth in these new industries is also more often an innovative environment coupled with venture capital, rather than tariff protection.

This option comes with a number of risks. The biggest danger is the inherently subjective nature of manually adopting reforms and the resulting potential for a fatal error to be made when prioritizing industries. Today's fastest growers (bio, nano, and info) may be replaced by other, more currently obscure, technologies, wasting the capital investment made in them. Development priorities made manually often simplify the economy to an extreme degree, and therefore drive support for undeserving producers. This option also requires significant financial resources, and a lack of domestic funds can necessitate external loans and foreign direct investment.

2) Protecting national interests

Manually implemented structural reforms can also be focused on national interests, or economic security for the country's development, as opposed to prioritized industries. Looking at the socio-economic sphere as a whole, they can be made up of a variety of industries: finance, energy, tech, ecology, foodstuffs, healthcare, education, and so on.

At the heart of this option lies a forecast of internal and external threats to those national interests. External threats are predicted by assessing how developed trade partners are, the global economy, and price levels for core imports and exports like gas, oil, and oil products. Internal threats depend on resource forecasts: human capital, finances, technology, water, and more.

There are risks that come with this option as well.

On the one hand, national security can take on such importance that it begins to encompass even areas that have traditionally been supported by the government (for example, the pharmaceutical industry or infrastructure).

On the other hand, subjective national interests can hog the spotlight to the extent that the government fails to intervene where the market is crumbling, be that public service, the shadow economy, or anything else.

It is important to underscore that determining national interests and threats to them is sufficient for security purposes but fails to secure growth for the country. Going beyond that could include improving human capital, infrastructure, state management, and technology.

Manual economic transformation assumes the deliberate creation of a parallel economic structure, and cultivating it, even at the cost of the old structure. It is that freedom from the old structure that creates an environment in which experiments, mistakes, and innovation are possible. New priorities, values, processes, and orders are established and used to select personnel. Most importantly, success in the context of the new structure is more likely than in the context of the old. A company's chances of achieving success when venturing out into new markets from 1976 to 1994 was 37%, as opposed to 6% when beginning within an old structure's existing markets.[121]

Manual reforms might sound pragmatic for the government. But in reality it's vice versa, and you never know what drives this visible hand of the state: ideology or culture (populism). Paul Collier, in his book, *The Future of Capitalism* writes that the ideologies of both left and right claim that context, prudence and practical reasoning can be bypassed by an all-purpose analysis spewing out truth valid for all contexts and all time. Populism offers an alternative bypass: charismatic leaders with remedies so obvious that they can be grasped instantly.[122]

Just as people create change for the better in their lives by finding a new job, going back to school, or moving to a higher paying industry, countries change the structure of their economy by focusing on their national interests and prioritizing promising industries. Certainly, the risks and transitional nature of this mechanism cannot be forgotten. It is also important to note that the paternalistic role the government plays is only temporary, and in the interests of attaining long-term benefits for society. However, if those benefits and the economic security the government promises do not materialize, it is time for the next transformation mechanism. Prosperity (primarily financial), or a lack thereof, is the yardstick by which this mechanism is judged, and the metric making it clear when to move on to the next mechanism, driving social demands and state support for a new economic policy.

The third mechanism: market-based structural reforms

This mechanism aims to create an environment in which long-term flexibility and economic stability are achieved by attracting private capital to the market. Predictable rules are what best draw private savings and investment while also promoting entrepreneurship, and so institutions (guaranteed property rights and the rule of law) and competitive markets are critical.

In practice, this mechanism can include a number of concrete structural reforms drawn from foreign experience, such as Russia's 500 Days Program, and the Balcerowicz Plan in Poland, and the recommendations of international financial organizations such as the IMF, the World Bank, and the EBRD:

A) Liberalized prices, trade, currency, and banking; a developed financial market;
B) Privatization, bankruptcy for noncompetitive companies along with targeted social support for those who lose their jobs in the process;
C) Streamlined public spending, lowered taxes and an expanded tax base, control over the budget deficit;
D) Reform for infrastructure as a whole, telecommunications, and electric energy; developed roads; utilization of water resources;
E) The creation of a favorable institutional climate for foreign and national investors that includes protection for property rights, cultivating competition, and improving corporate and state management;

On that foundation can be built a structure that is more country- and region-specific, though the core of transformation does not change. Speaking generally, this mechanism creates an unfettered economic structure that is driven by effective market practice rather than theories, preferences, and deductions. The main argument in its favor is that it is always worth leaving room for industries and outlets for development that simply cannot be known or predicted ahead of time. Even beyond that, the arrogance of scientists, politicians, and managers who supposedly know or can predict future priorities in a free structure are replaced by humility and adaptation to the power of a market that is utterly impossible to understand.

Structural reforms infuse the free market structure with flexibility by creating institutions; competitive markets for goods, labour, and capital; and the free flow of resources; equal access to financial resources, including state support, labour mobility, and more. Institutions, or the rules of the game, rather than the quality and professionalism of the players themselves, are what provide long-term stability for the free economic structure. Competition offers social security by protecting consumers from being at the mercy of sellers, workers from their employers, and the other way around. A free structure takes economics out of the hands of politicians, thereby creating balance.

Certainly, this mechanism has its risks:

1) A lack of priorities and a risk for national interests. Equal access to financial and other resources excludes manual transformation and the way it deliberately prioritizes the country's competitive advantages based on a scientific and technological forecast and analysis of national threats. It can also decrease current funding for social services like education and healthcare, casting doubt on the future development of human capital. Market-based structural reform is therefore best saved for areas in which national interests are not threatened.
2) The draw of falling back on old mechanisms. When institutions are weak, market-based structural reforms feel the urge to retreat into the welcoming embrace of old administrative habits. Discipline, and keeping a close eye on how structural reforms are affecting the market, are therefore critical. It is also important to have a strong controlling agency keeping the economy on a market track while institutions are being developed.

This mechanism and its specificities have been utilized in the past.

Central and Eastern Europe. As mentioned already, Polish, Czech, Slovak, and other models for market-based reform included privatization, bankruptcy for ineffective state-owned companies, liberalized prices, streamlined state expenditures and a smaller tax burden, and an emphasis on small and medium businesses.

These measures positively impacted life in those countries. From 1990 to 2007 (the start of the global financial crisis) there was strong correlation between the reforms that were instituted at the requirement of the EBRD and the UN's Human Development Index: from 0.8 to 0.99 in Bulgaria, Hungary, Poland, Slovenia, Slovakia, and the Czech Republic. In other words, the more energetically market-based structural reforms were pursued in those countries, the faster they developed.

Asia. The Chinese model of development and openness, which was in large part based on the experience of Singapore and Korea, in turn served as the roadmap for Vietnam and Myanmar. It was also the key to the third wave of development thinking, the core of which was contributed by Chinese economist and former Chief Economist at the World Bank, Justin Yifu Lin. He claimed that developing countries can take off if structural and national economic reform plays the lead role, informed throughout the process by global challenges.[123]

This model assumes gradual reform that moves from low-hanging fruit to more complex, experimental options. The Chinese model includes mutual openness between China and the rest of the world, a transfer of technology, and therefore copying and developing its own innovations. Growth rates of 8–10% were ultimately achieved, along with the largest currency stockpile in the world. The model even transformed the social sphere, brought on high social inequality, and introduced labour competition. The last few years have seen deepening structural reform, a prosperous middle class, the fight against corruption, and the rule of law added to China's economic strategy. At the same time, its economy has slowed to 6% growth, adding impetus to the need for jobs and social stability. The Chinese model is like a bicycle: the balance of stable social and economic development can only be maintained while reforms are pedalling forward.

It's necessary to add that some scholars warn us that in recent years Chinese state capitalism transforms not to market capitalism, but something different. In the book *The Age of Surveillance Capitalism,* by Shoshana Zuboff, it is claimed that a social responsibility system, with the help of IT, makes state capitalism invisible in China.[124] It navigates and defines human behavior, but the main decisions are still made by the state, and not the society or humans themselves. Information Technologies have become useful tools in the hands of the Chinese state to create a different mode of capitalism, as well as in the hands of big private corporations (platforms like Google, Facebook, Amazon, and Apple) in the USA. And the modern challenge is not uselessly to fight with IT, but to stand for the regulations and norms defending the individual rights, trust, and freedoms, of true capitalism.

General rules and mechanisms, the international experience of economic transformation, and the pitfalls facing state capitalism in Belarus all make reform unavoidable. A balanced, modest, look at the overall picture points to a path by which Belarus can find its new self, re-establish economic growth, and keep moving toward prosperity. That pragmatic path to overcoming what are basically financial pitfalls by increasing capital efficiency is the financial diet.

CHAPTER 6

THE FINANCIAL DIET

State capitalism reforms don't target the weakening of the state or to leave it with no money, relying only on national private and foreign financial inflows. Even in a market economy, the state plays an important role in different ways. In terms of public procurement, it is a buyer, and through competition between suppliers it organizes the construction of public buildings. As the legislative and executive power, it licenses influence on prices, and regulates monopolies. As the referee on the market it encourages competition and innovations, and limits the risks taken by financial organizations. But this is in a market economy. In a transition economy, the state can be both the player and the referee, the monopoly and competition watcher. So in order to push the state to take one role, it should have the exact amount of money required to do that, not more, not less. If it doesn't have enough financial resources to be the player or a monopoly, it will focus on the role of referee and legislator. Nowadays, the state has acquired the financial (not the only) power, and responsibilities that exceed its capacities, ones that can only be properly met by firms and local societies.

The financial diet refers to using set principles for distributing financial resources to create an environment in which state capitalism can be reformed. Those principles are macroeconomic stability, long-term financial equilibrium, and the effective use of public financial resources. Importantly, the financial diet is not a simple budget sequestration; instead, it is both a systemic reform of government finances and the conditions needed for economic transformation.

The first principle: macroeconomic stability

There is nothing more important when it comes to economic transformation than macroeconomic stability. Supported by a combination of monetary, budget, tax, and structural policy within an open economy, its target metrics are price levels and the nominal exchange rate. Speaking specifically of Belarus, there is a purely economic (theoretical) side to that coin, as well as a psychological (practical) side. Price and exchange rate stability have to be prioritized because of the country's financing deficit pitfall, which we looked at earlier, long-term inflation, historic devaluations, and the debt overhang.

Monetary policy is the key tool used to provide macroeconomic stability. Budget and tax policy conform to, and follow, its lead, meaning that the budget deficit and sources for financing it cannot push prices or the exchange rate higher. Even external financing of investment and the current account balance are subject to monetary policy in the context of an open economy. Finally, macroeconomic stability also requires structural policy tools that resolve the economic system into a new and mobile equilibrium supported by a balance between monetary, budget, and tax policy.

There are two roads to macroeconomic stability that monetary policy can take in Belarus: (a) use the exchange rate to manipulate prices, or (b) use the money supply to manipulate both prices and the exchange rate (given the fact that Belarusian inflation is driven by money emission). International practice also includes other, more complex, options utilized by countries with relatively developed market economies: inflation targeting, or targeting a hidden anchor (inflation-related or otherwise). Those strategies are better put on the back burner in Belarus in favor of one of the following options.

1) Option one: a fixed exchange rate

The experience of Bulgaria, Bosnia, Hong Kong, Lithuania, and Estonia shows that this can be strict and governed by a currency board. The money supply (M0 or M2) is legally pegged to reserves (foreign currency or gold), fixing the exchange rate, and money is only introduced by the central bank purchasing foreign currency. In other words, national currency only enters the economy via foreign currency used to purchase exports or finance foreign investment. Key to this option is a long-term commitment made either by introducing a new law, or as part of the banking code. Setting monetary policy in stone serves to build trust on the part of the various actors in the economy and narrow deflationary and inflationary expectations.

The advantages here are inflation that quickly drops below 10%, restored trust in the national currency, reduced deflationary and inflationary expectations, a greater propensity to save, and lowered long-term interest rates on loans. This option is preferred for, and made possible when, there are sufficient currency reserves to maintain a fixed exchange rate, and those are built up by the credit resources offered by international organizations as well as currency earned by privatization.

Among the disadvantages is the central bank's limited ability to extend credit to commercial banks. Without it, some poorly run banks could go bankrupt, as occurred in 1986 in Hong Kong, in 1992 in Lithuania, in 1994 in Estonia, and in 1995 in Argentina. Underfunded state financing programs push the burden for distributing financial resources onto the economy, revealing inefficient organizations, leading to some bankruptcies, and potentially eating into productivity, consumption, and growth. Interest rates on debt obligations denominated in the national currency grow in the short term, as they find equilibrium in the context of the new inflation rate. The long term could see deflation and/or default, and the related social upheaval, as per Argentina in 2002, if monetary policy conflicts with its budget and tax counterparts (if the deficit and debt increase hand in hand).

Of course, fixing the exchange rate means that it can no longer be used to boost the competitiveness of export prices. That is not a major concern in Belarus' case, however, given that prices for the country's main export goods (potash and oil products) are set by the global market, independent of the Belarusian rouble. The positive effect deflation might have on exports of non-raw materials is also mostly nullified by the higher cost of imported components. Ultimately, an oscillating Belarusian rouble offers more negative speculative and social consequences than would be outweighed by its economic benefits. A floating, market-based exchange rate is impossible in a non-market economy in which prices, interest rates, imports, labour, and other resources are regulated, so moving to, and maintaining, a floating rate can only occur once the transition has been made to a market economy. Any other sequence of events would lead to a drowning and unstable, if floating, rate.

International practice offers other types of fixed exchange rate policies that range from different degrees of fixation to built-in deviation, periodicity and conditions for when corrections are made. Regardless, having a currency board has proven to be the fastest way—taking 1–2 years—to stabilize the macroeconomy. For example, Bulgaria went from 578.5% inflation in 1997, when it established a currency board, to 1% in 1998 and 8.5% in 1999. Countries with a currency board enjoy lower rates of inflation than those employing other currency policies: from the

1970s to the 1990s, countries with a currency board saw inflation average 5% per year.[125]

This is a temporary path to macroeconomic stability. The currency board's goal is the eventual introduction of a new national currency, like the euro in the Baltics, or the creation of a fertile environment for financial economic and financial reform, as in Argentina and Bulgaria. Once the economic structure has adapted to the new conditions and competitive markets, and institutions have been created, forming a healthy financial climate, the transition to a more flexible, reactive, and stable exchange rate policy can begin.

2) Option two: a fixed rate of growth for the money supply

In this case the central bank sets limits for growth in the money supply (monetary targeting). For Belarus, that could be the rate of lending in the economy, given the outsized role it plays in the size of the money supply. The central bank would set lending parameters for banks, monitor them, and assign responsibility, though banks would be reduced to a level playing field and exemptions from capital requirements would be rescinded. This method for stabilizing inflation and the exchange rate has been successfully employed by the USA, Canada, and the UK. It was also policy for 20 years in Germany and Switzerland, beginning in 1974.

The main advantage this policy offers is that it is milder than the first option. Old state programs can be wound down, and limited economic growth can be maintained, though that comes at the cost of putting off stability for a total of 2–4 years. It also works well if reforms are accompanied by the parallel development of a new economic structure, as that changes deflationary and inflationary expectations as well as economic behavior.

The disadvantage is that inflation temporarily stays at 10–15%. The more flexible exchange rate policy also pushes prices higher, and deflationary and inflationary expectations can strengthen in the absence of clear signals pointing to reform. In that case, this monetary policy only keeps development in the public eye for a short time, sabotaging the transition from quantitative to qualitative economic growth. Higher inflation within the old structure accelerates solvency problems, as resources, manpower, and energy, are sapped. The tightened money supply in that situation creates a 'snowball' effect towards bankruptcy and social upheaval.

It is important to know that either of those two options is sufficient to introduce a degree of economic health, purge uncompetitive producers, and smooth out inflationary distortions. The difference is in how fast that occurs, and the effect the pace has on society. However, limiting policy to those two options, without also taking structural steps and implementing financial reforms, will push the economy into recession, which is why the issue of creating an environment in which old manufacturers can be wound down and new ones can be built up remains open. The problem is maintaining a free flow of financial, labour, information, material, and other resources from the old to the new. Put another way, that means the creation of fully-fledged and competitive markets for factors of production (capital, labour, and other resources), as well as their institutional framework. Macroeconomic stability is a critical, though not the only, condition for financial and economic transformation.

The second principle: long-term financial equilibrium

Macroeconomic stability and other financial reforms have to lead to long-term equilibrium for public finances. In other words, economic transformation must always take into account the government's foreign and domestic financial obligations (intertemporal budget constraints). Social obligations, public debt, and other expenses need to always be measured against expected revenue, and that is how long-term financial equilibrium is evaluated. That evaluation is straightforward, as long as the factors making up planned revenue and expenses are relatively predictable.

1) The government's long-term financial expenses generally include the following:
   1.1) Social welfare. The determining factors here are generally demographic trends reflecting the number and demographic makeup of state service consumers, as well as the costs associated with the birth rate, education, healthcare, and pensions.
   1.2) Government debt. In this case, the size and structure of the debt, in terms of the denomination, lender, due date, cost, and so on, are calculated. Access to refinancing at home and abroad, whether that be via the international capital market, international organizations, intergovernmental loans, or the stability of the domestic banking system, also plays a role.
   1.3) Infrastructure and security. The expenses involved in maintaining national security (including economic security) can be calculated by looking at long-term trends for maintenance

and replacement needed by transport, energy, and information infrastructure; social objects; the defense and healthcare industries; food and other raw resources; and so on. National security and government infrastructure are especially important when transforming state capitalism, because of the changing balance of power and interests between the public and private sectors.

2) The government's long-term revenue is generally made up of the following elements:
   2.1) Indirect taxes on consumption. Given the huge income they provide for the Belarusian budget, it is important to look at what drives them as well. Those drivers include trending changes in consumer demand, real income levels, tendencies to consume, and excisable goods, accounting for the steps the government takes to reduce alcohol consumption, smoking, and so on.
   2.2) Customs duties. Potential customs duties on exports are calculated by looking at changes in the global prices for raw materials such as oil and potassium. Import duties in Belarus can be calculated from the overall budget of the Eurasian Economic Community, as long as resource distribution and the growth rates of the participating countries are predictable.
   2.3) Direct taxes. Evaluating tax revenue from individuals and income tax revenue paid by legal entities over the long run can be done by looking at growth trends for labour productivity, potential GDP, possible policies aimed at boosting investment attractiveness, and the tax revenue they would drive.

Laying out time series for predicted revenue and expenses in a number of different scenarios related to, for example, prices on raw materials, clarifies the thresholds for the fiscal gap. With that said, a few assumptions are needed to build that model: the existing economic structure will remain in place, technology will remain the same, there will be no internal or external shocks, and inflation will be low. The forecast can be made more accurate by zooming in on the impact which separate factors, such as long-term financial obligations linked to demographic change, and public debt, have on financial equilibrium.

An aging population tends to be the primary reason why a long-term fiscal gap appears for many countries. Others expect future fiscal gaps due to demographic trends, growth rates for labour productivity, raw material reserves and prices, the level of government debt, currency reserves, and other factors. For example, by 2050, Russia will experience a fiscal gap that ranges from 13% to 14% of GDP, depending on the scenario. Of that number, 4.8% will be due to higher pension and medical entitlements. Greece, Belgium, Japan, and the USA anticipate a long-term fiscal gap amounting to 10% of GDP over the same period, with Finland reaching 8%, and Germany and Italy hitting 6%. Current estimates see the pension entitlements currently in place in Belarus driving a deficit of 1.8% of GDP in 2020, 3.6% in 2030, and 9% in 2050.

A number of conditions must be in place for long-term financial equilibrium to occur in Belarus.

First, government finances have to be divorced from those of state-owned enterprises.

For Belarus, that means separating the management and economic functions in the government finance system by imposing a limit on government intervention in the finances of state-owned companies, including via state support, providing government guarantees, subsidizing prices, and so on.

As a result, the government finance system would be left with separate areas characterized by long-term budget restraints:

A) National (resource) security: military (the military industrial complex); foodstuffs (part agriculture and part processing); resource (different parts potash, oil refining, resource creation, and meeting long-term needs); financial (part of the banking and insurance sectors); and so on. Certainly, resources are locked into the country's geographical area, meaning the government bears most of the responsibility for maintaining them. The private sector may be uninterested in helping, or limited in its ability to help, shoulder the responsibility for resources, possibly because it has the mobility to choose the country with the best and most plentiful selection of them.
B) The budget: state management, healthcare, education, science, law enforcement, and more. This area is social in scope and boasts multifaceted benefits, so it cannot simply be handed over to a private sector guided only by its own needs. Products here include scientific discoveries in medicine, ecology, or energy, and stripping it of state regulation can deplete the strategic reserves enjoyed by all of society. Gaps in healthcare or education in one tier of society drag other tiers down with them, and nullify investments being

made in unproductive areas. Here it is also important to set up limits for the services provided, in some cases free of charge, by the government. Interaction with the private sector should be made conditional on the government's need rather than private interests, and those interests should also serve as a signal to the government that it needs to review the limits of the influence it wields and expand public-private partnerships.

C) Natural monopolies (infrastructure): energy, railroads, air and other transport, and more. The government has the exclusive right to finance and regulate many types of infrastructure, and especially those like fuel and energy, utilities, roads, transport stations, airports, and ports that are universally needed. Handing those areas over to the private sector would create natural private monopolies that push prices for resources and infrastructure higher and restrict the pool of potential consumers. A state monopoly with its lower prices is, therefore, the more economic option.

State-owned and private enterprises falling outside those lines are resigned to free-floating competition. Financial intervention on the part of the government is therefore relegated to secondary importance, and only triggered by imbalance between industries. This could be, for example, the formation of a monopoly or capital that no longer flows freely from one industry to another, in either case meaning that equivalent capital no longer creates equivalent profit. New industries appear and are fought over by companies already in the market, and market capital often flows toward new industries that offer instant profit. Old industries begin to die out. The government intervenes in the resulting imbalance with temporary support for old industries or nationalization, also pushing their scientific and technological development in an effort to keep them from going completely obsolete and being replaced by imports. It also props up promising new industries that need investment. However, market demand needs to be the deciding factor when it comes to selecting which industries will receive state support. Synergetic interaction between industries means that the financial resources the government directs to both old and new industries find their way to the rest of the economy as well.

State-owned enterprises left to float freely should be given access to limited assistance, though that assistance should come with a requirement to maximize dividends. Chronically loss-producing companies should be put through bankruptcy proceedings and liquidated, while their smaller cousins, which the government has practically nothing to do with managing, and from which it receives practically nothing, can be privatized. That process can be implemented gradually.

The first step is inventorying all state-owned organizations held at the state, municipal, and other levels with sound criteria which the government needs for strategic reasons.

The second step is consolidating and concentrating state control over industry-specific and strategic corporations, leaving infrastructure (and companies maintaining local infrastructure) to municipal governments.

The third is to subject strategic, industry-specific corporations to the State Committee on Property, which will audit them and sign long-term contracts with their management which establish salaries, incentives, and responsibilities (the Chinese experience).

The fourth is to bankrupt, liquidate, or privatize small, medium-sized, and chronically insolvent companies. Large non-strategic companies, earmarked for liquidation, are distinguished from small companies, earmarked for privatization, by their return (the Central and Eastern European experience).

That way, the financial relationship between the government and all companies falling outside the lines drawn above is market- and competition-based, with all forms of ownership considered equally. The resulting long-term financial equilibrium enjoyed by the government will only include its own finances and those of narrowly defined state-owned enterprises.

Second, a financial market needs to be developed.

Letting a number of state-owned enterprises float freely without financial support in an environment financed by expensive bank loans necessitates a different source—a financial market. A financial market would also contribute to macroeconomic stability by lowering inflation: money would be invested in securities rather than goods and currency. The financial market can also be a transparent mechanism for privatization, though in Belarus it is not up to the job: in 2013 stock market capitalization to GDP was 0.7%, and bond capitalization to GDP was around 20%. By way of comparison, in Russia those numbers were 40% and 22%, in Ukraine 21% and 35%, and in China 50% and 41%.

Cultivating the financial market in Belarus requires a number of steps to be taken simultaneously. Half-measures, hanging onto manual management, allowing local authorities preference when it comes to buying shares, withdrawing profits, and directed sales of stock would all destroy the system as well as the trust of investors. The steps needed to develop the financial market in Belarus are:

1) Creating a traditional corporate management structure at state-owned companies complete with supervisory boards, directors, shareholders, and guaranteed rights for all of them.
2) Publishing reports and balance sheets in an effort to open up more information. Data provided on stock exchange sites must be straightforward and accessible to the target users. If the financial market is primarily geared towards foreign investors, it needs to be understandable for them and resemble something they are used to. For example, Armenia and the Baltic states sold their exchanges to the NASDAQ, which implemented cutting-edge technology and the information standards foreign investors are accustomed to.
3) Issuing blue-chip stock in 5–6 strong companies with revenue streams, strong reputations, and good prospects. Those companies could be in telecommunications or energy, or they could be retail chains or banks—the key is to gain experience creating special investment funds used to grow those types of companies and issue their stock on the financial market. For example, Kazakhstan has Samruk-Kazyna, a Sino-Kazakhstani sovereign wealth fund.
4) Adopting additional legislation that makes financial assets more attractive, unlocks new tools, and guarantees investor rights. Most important is legislation on depository notes, investment funds, and long-term tax breaks for bond earnings. Kazakhstan's creation of a financial center that uses the English language, as well as English law and judges, is an intriguing example of how to protect shareholder and investor rights.
5) Creating a central regulatory body. Banks, insurance companies, and professionals all participate in the financial market, which could enjoy fraud-free independent monitoring. Many countries—Russia, Kazakhstan, Singapore, the Czech Republic, and Canada, for example—base their regulators in their central banks.

Third, the government needs to fulfill its long-term monetary obligations.

Financial equilibrium can only be achieved in an open Belarusian economy with a significant currency deficit if the government fulfills its domestic and foreign debt obligations. Currency reserves, the current account balance, foreign direct reserves, and new foreign currency-denominated borrowing are all ways funding could be found to meet that goal.

The importance of accumulating and maintaining currency reserves at a safe level, and only paying for government obligations using funds over and above that level, is worth stating separately. The IMF puts it equal to three months of imports, and that number could be achieved in Belarus' case by privatizing state property such that the government would receive foreign currency in return—for example, by issuing stock in state-owned enterprises on foreign capital markets.

Belarus' foreign currency-denominated debt has a few features that bear mentioning.

The first is a foreign currency-denominated return. The debt taken out by the government in foreign currency unrelated to investment projects should, first and foremost, drive a foreign currency-denominated return by stimulating exports and foreign direct investment. In some cases, it could also be used to build up reserves in the interests of macroeconomic stability or to refinance older foreign currency-denominated debt. With that said, even foreign currency-denominated debt and guarantees taken out and made by the government related to investment projects should come with a requirement that the return be denominated in foreign currency so as to avoid payment coming out of the budget (as opposed to from the project).

The second is new creditors. Switching from foreign creditors to their more expensive domestic counterparts could be one way of refinancing Belarus' old foreign currency-denominated debt, though that would push government debt higher. Externally refinancing debt is another option, though in that case it is critical to diversify creditors in order to maintain maneuverability. In either case, the growth in public debt that changing creditors would entail cannot exceed refinancing rates.

The third is new borrowers. The corporate debt taken out by state-owned enterprises and banks within state capitalism is often guaranteed by the government. Even the non-guaranteed loans they take out often enjoy a secret guarantee, given that creditors associate them with the government. The combination of secret and open guarantees saps financial discipline and pushes public debt, including the financial obligations of state-owned companies, higher over the long run. As a result, in reality, a switch to new borrowers occurs when the government begins managing debt taken out by the entire public sector as well as its own. The process also becomes more politicized. At the same time, economic instruments like syndicated loans and sovereign, municipal, and corporate bonds are underutilized.

Foreign currency-denominated public debt can only be better managed and depoliticized by divorcing it from the government. Practically speaking, the best institutional option would be handing management of government debt over to the Development Bank. Austria, Belgium, the UK, Hungary, Ireland, France, Sweden, and other countries, all have separate agencies charged with managing public debt; in Belarus' case the Development Bank could take control and compete with transnational investment banks for international capital on behalf of the government. That control would not even have to include assuming the balance of the debt, as the Development Bank would simply handle planning, bringing in new funds, monitoring, paying it off, and so on. That would help to increase how well projects guaranteed by the government, and therefore associated with external public debt, are evaluated, and improve the operations of those not guaranteed by the government with better risk management. The government can make a single state entity, for instance, the National Bank, responsible for the Development Bank and all foreign currency-denominated reserves.

And that is how long-term financial equilibrium could be achieved in Belarus: by divorcing public finances from those of state-owned companies, setting up a financial market, and better managing foreign currency-denominated public debt.

The third principle: better use of public financial resources

Public finances use government services to redistribute financial resources, and the public finance system is therefore geared towards providing its clients with the best and highest quality services possible. With that in mind, moving the government away from manual management, where it offers financing to meet current needs, and towards program-specific financial services, where it gives government agencies medium-term goals to meet, is key.

That kind of transformation focuses primarily on spending: results-oriented budgeting. Every item in the budget has to come with a concrete result. Within that mindset, however, social benefits (education, healthcare, science, culture) deserve the spotlight, given the primary role they play in the future of the country. That is more than just boosting income and offering more access to financing, however; it means streamlining public spending by giving organizations the freedom to choose the type of financing that best meets their needs. Higher incomes are also not out of the question, though they are most likely reserved for those who make the largest contribution to the overall result. This type of reform would see new approaches to budget administration and control implemented, more trust placed in company directors, and the disappearance of money ("you can't spend on pens because it was earmarked for pencils"). It would also affect the local authorities nearest to government service consumers. In fact, it is exactly those local authorities who are privy to the most information about the needs of the people, and can best react to, and satisfy emerging needs. Expanding the financial independence they enjoy, and strengthening interregional equality, would ensure equal access to social services for everyone who needs them.

This transformation would also affect revenue. Tax services need to be subject to the same requirements placed on other government services: simplicity, speed, and stability. The new elements for Belarus would be adding more information, possibly streamlining fiscal agencies, adopting state economic paternalism, and adding tax consulting services. The key is landing on an approach to deviations, such as tax breaks and preferential treatment, that mirrors the evaluation, control, and reporting required of public spending. Of course, any reform that requires rebuilding the tax system needs to also include a tax amnesty.

There are several main areas where this method for altering the public finance system plays out.

First, a new ideology for public finances.

This involves moving away from control and distribution toward results-oriented services, or offering the key government services included in collecting and allocating the government's financial resources. The difference is, that this switches the focus from the financial services provided to the government services through which they are provided. Those services can then be consolidated and tied into specific programs with separate priorities for financing. Concrete target metrics, met with the help of the financial resources handed out by the government, could also be used to assess the performance of each service. The government agency providing each service would decide where to spend its funds on its own, as it would be incentivized to get the best return and meet its target metrics.

Belarus began implementing a program-specific method in the early 2000s, and from 2009 to 2015 program expenses stayed below 25% of all expenditures. At the same time, the number of programs financed from the state budget grew from 60 in 2009 to 78 in 2014. The primary funds were concentrated in the country's agricultural complex (around 45%), followed by the Road of Belarus program (12%), and the expenses involved in cleaning up after the Chernobyl disaster (11%).

Some problems with results-oriented budgeting are:

1) Programs do not always lend themselves to efficiency metrics. Many simply do not have them: out of 87 analyzed programs, 35 do not (more than 40%).
2) Some programs feature poorly chosen efficiency metrics, and the systems they do have sometimes do not match their project objectives. In most cases this is due to a lack of clearly formulated goals.
3) Program planning is not always built on analysis of results in previous periods. As a rule, money is allocated based on the amount appropriated in past years rather than on the metrics that have been reached. A shortage of funds sometimes means that even allocated money never makes it to its designated programs. Problems also arise when the time comes to forecast results and expenses over a program's life, something that is especially difficult for long-term programs.
4) There is no effective way to exert interim control over programs from the inside on the part of the coordinating client. The only tool in place is a yearly review of reports received from all programs. An enormous number of the reports received do not correspond to their requirements.
5) There is no method for effectively implementing programs. Metrics measuring efficiency and results are developed by interested ministers and agencies, meaning that they are often formal and poorly designed tools for making management decisions.

New Zealand is an example of this approach. Its Better Public Services plan includes ten specific goals for government services over the coming five years. Brazil is also an interesting case, as it built its three-year plan on an average of 10–12 metrics handed down to each ministry, which are then assigned in turn to different employees. The salary and career prospects of each public servant depend directly on their performance, as measured by those metrics. An updated law was adopted in the US in 2010 with metrics used to evaluate government agencies, this time adding criteria for assessing government employees to the original law passed in 1993.

Second, longer planning periods for public finances.

This goes for the country's entire financial balance, and includes setting up long-term assessments, enacting medium-term budgets, and managing those budgets. Indicative forecasting needs to be worked into the national planning system in a way that provides for rolling medium-term predictions; long-term predictions for fiscal, monetary, and other macroeconomic metrics; maximum spending that does not exceed projected revenue; and medium-term goals.

There are some elements of medium-term planning built into the Belarusian budget code. For instance, Article 86 dictates the development of a medium-term (three-year) financial program.

However, that is not done in practice, given the lack of a legislative framework for medium-term forecasting, well-grounded macroeconomic prognoses, clear budget goals, and metrics for measuring the efficiency of public spending. There is also no standard for a three-year budget (not to mention a medium-term financial program). The absence of rolling forecasts, coupled with budgetary legislation that is changed asynchronously, has made it impossible to implement a medium-term system for budget planning. Marginal costs matching predicted revenue and medium-term goals are also not in place.

Malaysia is a good example here. In 1991, it announced its Vision 2020 strategy, aimed at boosting GDP and living standards, promoting a self-sufficient economy, and developing a political system. The country was able to attain a certain level of economic development thanks to that strategy, which was sometimes even taken outside the system, in the face of regional and global financial crises. Kazakhstan, China, Sweden, and other countries, also have similar long-term strategies.

Third, promoting financial independence for local authorities.

This is especially important for federated and unitary countries with a few large, economically significant administrative units. Promoting self-dependence for federal unities or local authorities boosts their economic independence and their contribution to the country's overall economic growth. The largest taxes would therefore be paid at the local or regional level, rather than at the state or federal levels. Financial self-dependence would go a long way towards solving economic and social disconnects at the local level, underpin stability for the country as a whole, and boost how fast and how well government services are provided, given the fact that local authorities are physically much closer to the recipients of those services.

As market relationships are built in Belarus and the economic structure is altered, the role of regional authorities needs to be bolstered in order to counteract weakened industry management. The strategic objective is to implement mechanisms for cluster-based growth and growth points in the regional economy. However, those should lean more towards complex system-building regional projects set up in different areas, rather than simply setting up lone-wolf enterprises.

The readiness of Belarusian society for a high degree of local independence is the environment needed to develop regional self-governance. At this stage, that includes local authorities who should develop partnerships with local society and public organizations as part of a plan for regional development. That plan should be built on new mechanisms: public-private partnerships, state social orders, and projects aimed at fostering local initiatives, among others.

Local budgets have the following tools for widening their revenue base:

First, they can develop a local budget model that recommends parameters for them and regulates revenue and transfers (subsidies and subventions). It would also limit subsidies in local budgets and set a minimum level for its own revenue.

Second, they could expand the jurisdiction of local authorities in an effort to bring in more revenue. For instance, they could issue municipal bonds on international financial markets.

Third, they can optimize the cash flows between the different levels in the budgetary system by developing a system of funds for regional recipients and donors (relative to the federal budget). Local budgets could also bring their own revenue bases in line with the spending powers enjoyed by local authorities. Global practice holds that all levels of the budget system should support at least 70% of their total with their own revenue.

Fourth, boosting the role played by tax services.

The way the capital and the government interact in today's world engenders problems that impact both the distribution of added value in particular, and human development overall. Fiscal policy is the tool countries have to manage economic growth, and it is important to note that direct taxation is the fairest kind for society. Real taxpayers are, in that case, capital owners rather than consumers. On the other hand, sticking to direct taxation is only an option for developed countries. Lower income levels for individuals and corporations, as well as poor tax discipline, and the stable source of revenue it provides, are all factors in favor of indirect taxation for developing countries. Still, direct taxation is the best tool for the government and capital once income levels, living standards, and the tax base all grow. It should be noted that taxation is a burden borne more by individuals than corporations. With that in mind, the focus needs to be on setting up the infrastructure needed to provide quality tax services for individuals.

In 2014, tax revenue, plus payments into the Social Protection Fund, made up 36.6% of GDP. Unfortunately, the tax burden in Belarus is bumping up against its ceiling: pushing tax rates higher would not lead to a commensurate growth in tax revenue, and would instead have a number of negative side-affects. Tax increases in 2013 and 2014 did lead to growth in tax revenue in 2013, but that trend reversed itself the next year. In 2012, the tax burden was 36.7%, in 2013 it was 38.1%, and in 2014 it was 36.6%. Because of that, the search for a solution to the budget deficit has to turn towards better use of existing resources, a goal best served by implementing a long-term moratorium on tax increases, and thereby facilitating a stable tax policy.

Interlaced and complementary normative acts at different levels, and in different areas, dilute their impact and utility. Transparency, simplicity, and accessibility would be better served by implementing a single direct-action legal document that covers all tax-related issues: a tax code. Russia has paved the way in this regard by automatically including all of its legislation that includes tax-related issues in the country's tax code. The primary and best way to reduce the time spent by taxpayers would be to create a website where they can manage their taxes, make social payments, get information, participate in surveys, and more.

Elements of state paternalism could also be a new way to administer tax services, by interfering in the lives of the citizenry against their will, but in the interests of bettering their condition. Taxation could be the primary focus of that type of paternalism, equipped as it is by both harsh and more easy-going tools. The harsher tools at its disposal are focused on limiting and prohibiting, and they include high taxes on gambling, ecologically damaging manufacturing, alcohol and tobacco consumption, and more. More easy-going tools prompt and incentivize, and are generally focused on tax universality and developing social norms, culture, and the 'ideal' taxpayer. Soft paternalism is exemplified by the fiscal agencies in the UK, which post lists of tax dodgers on their sites and send newsletters to their neighbors in order to shame them in the public arena. Another option is developing a mechanism for public control over the taxes paid by businesses and public servants via online and print media, forums, and a trust service, though that would have to include taking responsibility for the accuracy of the information provided.

A receipt lottery is an example of tax-based paternalism in which store receipts also serve as lottery tickets. These incentivize customers to take receipts, and sellers to scan their goods. In Armenia, the expenses associated with the receipt lottery amounted to 10 million dollars, though the additional revenue it brought in was 30 million dollars. Over the three years, a receipt lottery was held in Tver Oblast, Russia, and tax revenue grew by 15% annually. The first year of the receipt lottery in Georgia saw the amount of business conducted by a population of 4.5 million people grow by 56 million dollars. Receipt lotteries have also led to growth in the tax revenue brought in by Azerbaijan, China, Turkey, and the Philippines.

An experimental receipt lottery was held in Belarus in December 2014, with an eye towards stimulating consumption, boosting financial awareness, and increasing taxes. The Kupalovskiy and Partizanskiy shopping centers in Minsk, and the Secret shopping center in Gomel, ran advertising campaigns entitled "Receipts: your lucky ticket", and "It's our little secret: your receipt is your lucky ticket". The gist of the game was that receipts doubled as lottery tickets.

As it turned out, the timing for the receipt lottery could have been better. In December 2014, deflationary expectations and instability in the financial market saw sales drop at most shopping centers. Still, those participating in the advertising campaign, with the exception of the Secret shopping center, noted an upward tick in proceeds, as compared to their competitors.

Fifth, transforming state control over economy.

This means going from control over state financial resources to monitoring how well state services are administered, something that requires a new system for intermediate state control, metrics broken down by year, and new intermediate and final reporting. That way, financing could be held back when it is not driving acceptable results. Penalties would be for failing to adequately provide government services, as measured by the metrics in place, rather than for using financial resources other than for their intended purpose.

Systems for state control should focus not on catching as many violators as possible, but on streamlining regulations. Considering the fact that people do business honestly for the most part, the large number of violators speaks to poorly set up regulations that cannot but be violated. The goal of reducing that number would be better served by a system for state control that suggests ways to improve the regulatory framework.

Some of the ways state agencies are controlled in Belarus are duplicates of each other. That is particularly true when it comes to monitoring tax and financial agencies (the different structures within the State Control Committee of the Republic of Belarus), customs agencies (the structures within the State Customs Committee of the Republic of Belarus), and the Ministry of Labour and Social Protection. International practice features many ways to streamline fiscal agencies.

Estonia has a Tax and Customs Board that includes a tax department (methodology), a customs management department (developing customs policy and handling customs duties), a monitoring department (organizing and running inspections), and an investigatory department (handling investigations, pre-trial and otherwise, of tax and customs offenders).

Latvia has its State Revenue Service that combines financial inspections and a customs department. The service's three key departments are run by the deputy directors for customs, the tax area, and the area of combating crime.

Armenia collected its fiscal organs under the umbrella of the Ministry of Finance. Different deputy ministers of finance are responsible for the budget and tax process, customs, and investigations and pre-trial procedures, each of which has its built-in subdivision responsible for developing financial policy.

Kazakhstan's Ministry of Finance includes a customs committee, a tax committee, and a finance committee tasked with fighting money laundering and terrorism.

The EU has its own examples. For instance, the Netherlands has its Tax and Customs Administration, while Hungary has its National Tax and Customs Administration.

The system for monitoring public services in Belarus also needs to do a better job giving society a more active role. That could be done, for example, by expanding the information published in budgetary reports for different levels of government. Opinion polls and studies are also essential ways the public can weigh in on how well the government is providing and financing public services.

Sixth, staffing.

Who does one delegate reforms to? Who knows how, and is able to work differently? Are there enough public servants with western (market-oriented) education and experience? Wearing western clothes does not even necessarily point to a western way of thinking; speaking foreign languages and living with a western flair are not a sufficient background for running structural reform. Belarus needs western intellectuals, tech experts, engineers, financiers, and economists. However, once they get here they will still have to interact with the existing apparatus, businessmen, and law enforcement agencies—the old Soviet guard. Low salaries and a lack of prestige involved in working for the government also pushes public servants into the private sector, keeping them from developing a new strategy. They have no incentive to work towards a new strategy they cannot see a place in for themselves.

Developing and implementing new methods is something that cannot be done without scientists, experienced foreign specialists, and representatives of the Ministry of Finance and industry departments. That, in turn, requires a scientific base that can offer basic and advanced training, though for that the staffing policy in place for the state apparatus would have to move away from its focus on bringing in highly educated workers. China, Kazakhstan, Russia, and Singapore are all examples of countries that have set up training for current and potential government employees at leading educational institutions abroad. For instance, in December 2013, a directive was signed in Russia, according to which the government would pay for the education of 3,000 students (1,000 each year for the next three years) who were able to get into graduate programs at the world's top universities. In return for the federal funding they received, they agreed to work for the Russian government for three years after graduation. If they failed to do so, the government would have rescinded the stipend and charged a fine that amounted to twice its value.

There is one thing worth discussing when it comes to the issue of paying for potential government employees to be educated abroad: this type of long-term approach works best when there are both administrative and market-based incentives to return home and take a position in the government. Those are generally social status, a guaranteed job, social benefits (preferential healthcare, education, housing, transportation, food, and a pension), and a moderate, fair, and competitive salary.

The market competitive salary is sometimes crucial in attracting talented people to the civil service. Otherwise, we see the widespread examples of a 'revolving door' through which public officials obtain jobs in the companies they once regulated. The classic case of how to deal with that is Singapore. Public sector salaries are pegged to the prevailing market in order to maintain public sector competitiveness for the best available domestic employers. The salaries of senior civil servants are pegged at two-thirds the median salaries of the top 48 earners in 6 professions: accounting, banking, engineering, law, local manufacturing firms and multinational corporations.[126] As a result, the salary of a Singaporean Minister is around 1.5 million dollars per year.

There are two notes that apply to Belarus' case in particular when it comes to switching over to a service-based system for public finances that keeps an eye on the quality of government services, and therefore, all of the state apparatus and the management decisions it makes.

The first is that this approach offers a way to manage finances—manually or by working toward targets. Before that question can be answered in Belarus, however, answers to the questions of what there is to manage, and in what areas, need to be worked out. In other words, as has already been mentioned, the first thing to do is disassociate government finances from those of state-owned enterprises. Only then can goals and metrics be imposed on the government finance system. Jumping straight to the second issue without resolving the first could put the different systems at odds with each other, disorientate government agencies, and keep their focus on avoiding mistakes instead of on their work. Belarus, therefore, needs a multi-step strategy that temporarily includes two parallel management systems. All that takes time, manpower, and money.

The second is the importance of accounting for inertia and kick-backs from existing personnel, necessitating a different way of motivating public servants, incentivizing them to perform to the new metrics, and focusing all new hiring on meeting concrete needs. There is also a risk of jumping into the opposite ditch to what we have today: government employees so focused on meeting their medium-term goals that they ignore the problems in front of them. Ultimately, implementing this approach demands willpower, control, and discipline, all while avoiding duplicated, split, and delegated, authority between executive, monitoring, law enforcement, and other agencies.

The last decade has seen a generational shift in Belarus' state apparatus, with younger ministers, deputies, and directors coming onto the scene. However, since 2013, the government and the central bank (regardless of who has been in charge) have kept up continuous programs aimed at structural reform. This points to both a generational shift, and a mentality shift, at the middle levels. At the same time, while there may not be a clear vision for a new economic structure, there are obviously problems with the old one. Each year the same reforms are developed more and more often in response to economic problems, and their critical mass is only growing.

CONCLUSION

State capitalism in the case of Belarus is a mobilized economic model with a number of characteristics.

First. It evolved under the influence of many objective, subjective, internal, and external factors. In Belarus, they include: the country's Soviet heritage, the crisis of an economy in transition, social support for a socialist government during the instability of the 1990s in neighboring countries, and financial influxes from outside the country.

Second. State capitalism in Belarus is a model of a transition economy. It differs from Central and Eastern European shock therapy, as well as from the Chinese version of gradualism, without focused structural reforms (or at least without declaring them). At the same time, the structure of the Belarusian economy has changed naturally (the services and private sectors have grown) under the influence of both global and regional processes strictly unrelated to management decisions made with transformation in mind. Ultimately, structural change in Belarus has been subtle, has not contradicted the country's ideology, and has managed to remain attached to state capitalism.

Third. State capitalism in Belarus can only function with public support at its back. That support is based on a number of factors, the first being social equality and income growth (that stopped in 2015). Periodic macroeconomic shocks and inflation caused by expanding the money supply have restrained the formation of a strong middle class with its demands for institutional change. The second factor is social security provided by jobs at state-owned enterprises. The third is the economy's socialist bent, which has driven a high tax burden and consolidated budgetary resources.

Fourth. State capital in Belarus has been accumulated primarily through the use of market tools like banks with foreign capital and private businesses. At the same time, state capitalism in Belarus leans on less market-based tools: state-owned enterprises (especially in the primary sector), state banks, the Development Bank, and the National Development Fund. The general mechanism for managing those instruments is administrative, an approach that, especially for state organizations, includes setting goals, directing credit, budget support, and utilizing the government's administrative resource. That has been sufficient to provide short-term momentum, though over the long term it has supplanted initiative and inflated operational expenses.

Fifth. State capitalism might be appropriate when it comes to handling short-term issues. Drawn from that is an assumption that it also works well over the long term, and that is why the current economic structure has remained in place. However, the push to hang onto the current model limits its flexibility and focuses it exclusively on handing out and following up on orders, inflating the influence over the economy enjoyed by control and law enforcement.

Sixth. The path to investment growth for state capitalism in Belarus has its pitfalls: the inflationary pressure and debt overhang that have accumulated limit the government's ability to rebuild its capital and finance the economy in general. Conflicts between neighboring countries eat away at international trade and FDI. Lack of innovation locks the country in the 'middle-income' trap. High social expenditures and relatively high income levels squeeze the budget and the national economy's competitiveness. The way the economy is naturally restructuring means changes are needed in the management system, and moving away from a focus on raw materials impacts currency reserves and the budget. That kind of environment slows even naturally occurring economic transformation, reins in growth, and drops the country farther behind others with more adaptive economic structures.

Analyzing how Central and Eastern Europe, the CIS, and China have approached structural economic reform yields a number of conclusions.

(a) Post-Soviet countries experienced reform in two stages: adaptation and development. The degree to which the first was necessary depended on the depth of the problems they were facing—in other words, whether or not they had the internal reserves needed for transformation. That stage featured a spike in inflation, labour, and financial mobility, and an influx of foreign direct investment, primarily in privatization projects. The speed at which Central and Eastern European countries moved through the second stage—development—depended on external stimuli, and especially on entrance into the EU. Drooping economies, the geopolitical influence of Russia, and the economic influence of China have served as stimuli for CIS countries. The development stage features a resolution to inflation problems as well as sustained unemployment and labour mobility. A lack of transparency has made reformists unpopular, raising alternative notions of nation building, populism, and conservatism as ways for politicians to hold onto power. Ultimately it halted, or even reversed, the ongoing transformation, dragging some economies into recession.

(b) One thing that stands out about Chinese reforms is that, while at first glance they seem unique, further study and a larger view of global experience prove them to be much more recognizable. The sheen of Chinese specificity wears off, and the conclusion that remains is that there is actually nothing unique about the Chinese experience. History lays out the standards, technologies, and practices that pave the road to the market economy, and China simply took that road, adapted, followed the rules to the letter, and leveraged its advantages to become a world leader. China's main reforms coincided historically with those of Central and Eastern Europe and the CIS: the first real attempts toward economic transformation were made at the end of the 1980s. The 1990s saw prices liberalized, privatization, and the main flow of foreign direct investment. In the 2000s, countries began investing abroad on their own, and the current decade has been spent overcoming the aftershocks of the global financial crisis and getting back to growth. In other words, economic reform moved forward under the simultaneous influence of both internal and external factors. On the other hand, China differs from European and post-Soviet countries in that it has internal incentives for economic transformation, and they serve both to discipline the country and push it faster along the path of development. With that said, traditional centralized decision-making in China does come with risks that jeopardize steady long-term growth. Centralization and the role personality plays can lead to development in a variety of directions: from the Cultural Revolution and Great Leap Forward to the policy of reform and opening.

It is important to emphasize that economic transformation is an orderly and logical process subject to a number of rules: priorities determine the strategy, the strategy determines the structure, and the structure determines the personnel.

There are three mechanisms for reforming state capitalism. The first is to simply let the old structure run its course. However, as the system gets more complicated, it gets harder to evaluate the probability and risk of systemic collapse. The second choice is to implement structural reform manually by economic emulation and protecting specific national interests. The problem here is that space is created for critical mistakes to be made when the going gets tough. The third option, a market-based implementation of structural reforms, does not guarantee an easy path; on the other hand, it is practical and based on the experience of countries with varying cultures, in different stages of development, and even on different continents (Europe and Asia).

All of the above nudges Belarus toward change. Pragmatically speaking, the best way to overcome the pitfalls to and bring back economic growth is to increase capital efficiency. That path is called the financial diet. It includes optimally distributing public financial resources in an effort to achieve macroeconomic stability by accumulating foreign reserves and targeting the exchange rate. It means long-term financial equilibrium (decreasing the fiscal gap) and a results-oriented focus for public financial services. It leads to financial independence for state-owned enterprises. It even touches on state, as well as local, budgeting, strategic planning, tax services, and improving state control. Bringing in professionals is key.

The financial diet is not austerity, as state capitalism in Belarus cannot exist without capital. On the other hand, budgetary resources do have to be limited in order to avoid constant depreciation, inflation, and the need for more public debt. The external environment in which the country finds itself, threatens it with long-term stagnation, underlining the importance of legal order and both fiscal and monetary discipline. Unfortunately, that is not enough. The financial diet, which is just the beginning, therefore also includes a variety of sources Belarus can use to replenish its capital via private and foreign investment.

The financial diet is a way to point out what is efficient, and who works well, in state capitalism. If you lack the ability to distinguish between facts and desires, it will bring you to authoritarianism. As Timothy Snyder puts it, in the epilogue of his book *The Road to Unfreedom,* the cynic who sees no truth is the citizen who welcomes the tyrant.[127] The financial diet is the way to distinguish figures, facts, and truth, that encourage trust in the economy and revive its growth.

ACKNOWLEDGEMENTS

This book was written in 2015 as a stressful reaction to economic recession in Belarus. Working as Economic Advisor to the President of the Republic of Belarus, I felt it was necessary to share responsibility for the downturn. So I put the words on paper for the public to read, as I didn't manage to knock them into the minds of the decision makers, for them to implement. That's how this book has become an open report.

It would have been impossible to write this book without the support of my family – my wife Elena and my two sons, Anton and Ilya. This book was written on their shoulders, their tolerance, and their silence. So, it is dedicated to them.

The first edition of this English version was published in 2016 with the support of the UNDP team: Sanaka Samarasinha and Ekaterina Paniklova.

Earlier in 2015, a more detailed Russian version of this book was published in Belarus. Whereas this pocket version in English is designed to help foreigners to understand the Belarusian economy, the longer Russian version is for Belarusians who want to understand how to improve it. Belarusian readers, fellow public servants, and journalists pushed the Russian book to an unexpected place on the list of best-selling business publications in Belarus.

Thank you also to everyone who read and commented on the manuscript: Mikhail Golosov, Dimitri Gvindadze, Sergey Guriev, Courtney Fingar, Ben Slay, Dmytro Sologub, Yuri Tserlukevich.

In 2020, this updated and revised version went public. I didn't have to change a lot of the section about Belarus. The conclusions are the same. But I had to update the chapter about Chinese experience. And this was not only because I spent more than three years there recently, but because it was worth writing about, as it's been changing. So, last but not least, I would like to thank everyone who make changes (reforms, transformations, transitions). That's what makes life unpredictably beautiful.

Kiryl Rudy
August 2020

NOTES

1 The term 'manual management' is a translation from Russian, and refers to an economic model in which the government deals with issues on a case-by-case basis, instead of allowing norms, systems, and structures to work by themselves.
2 Aven P. (2015). The USSR was a dangerous country, not like Russia today. (In Russian) [Electronic resource] // https://slon.ru
3 With the fall of the Soviet Union, the government reverted to a crisis mode of operating, managing a number of large and small crises across different sectors of the economy and society.
4 Guriev S. (2014). Myths of Economics: Fallacies and Stereotypes Spread by the Media and Politicians. (In Russian) — 5th ed. — Moscow: Mann, Ivanov and Ferber, 2014. — Pp 320.
5 Unless otherwise noted, currency is expressed in USD.
6 Scheidel W. (2017). The Great Leveler. Violence and the History of Inequality from the Stone Age to the Twenty-First Century. – Princeton University Press. Princeton, 2017. – 504 p.
7 Acemoglu D., Robinson J. (2006). Economic Origins of Dictatorship and Democracy. — Cambridge University Press, 2006.
8 Ibid.
9 Levitsky S., Way L. (2010). Competitive Authoritarianism: Hybrid Regimes after the Cold War (Problems of International Politics). — Cambridge University Press, 2010.
10 Aven P. (2015). The USSR was a dangerous country, not like Russia today. (In Russian) [Electronic resource] // https://slon.ru
11Based on the data from Ministry of Taxes and Levies of Belarus // http://www.nalog.gov.by
12Piketty T. (2014). Capital in the Twenty-First Century. — Belknap Press, 2014.
13 Li Ch. (2016). Chinese Politics in the Xi Jinping Era: Reassessing Collective Leadership. – Washington: Brookings Institution Press, 2016. – 512 p.
14 Based on the data from the National Statistical Committee of the Republic of Belarus. – http://www.belstat.gov.by
15 Based on the data from the Ministry for Taxes and Levies of Belarus, and Belstat.
16 Narivonchik D. (2020). Unexpected Statistics on Belarusian State Sector. No Reforms, but Something Happening. (In Russian) – http://www.neg.by
17Lobodanova D. (2014). Strategies for Developing Old Industrial Cities (In Russian) // Voprosy Economiki. — 2014. — № 4. — Pp. 56–76.
18 Nekipelov A. (2014) On Effectively Disposing of State Assets: Continuing the Development of an Alternative Strategy for Russian Socio-Economic Development as Begun by Scientists of the Economic Section at the RAN Social

Sciences Department (In Russian) // Russian Journal of Economics. — 2014. — № 2. — Pp. 3–21.

19 Radigin A., Simachev Y., Entov R. (2015). The State-Owned Company: State or Market Failures? (In Russian) // Voprosy Economiki. — 2015. — № 1. — Pp. 45–79.

20Banking Sector, as of April 1, 2020. // The National Bank of the Republic of Belarus / http://www.nbrb.by

21 Ibid.

22 Shmarlovskaya G., Petrushkevich E. (2010) International Investment in Sovereign Funds for National Welfare (In Russian) // Bankovsky Vestnik. — 2010. — № 25. — Pp. 35–41.

23 IMF (2010). Republic of Belarus: Selected Issues. January 2010. IMF Country Report No. 10/16. IMF. Washington, D.C.

24 Kruk D., Bornukova K. (2014). Belarusian Economic Growth Decomposition (In Russian) / BEROC Working Paper Series. — Working Paper No. 24. — Pp. 39.

25Based on the data from the National Statistical Committee of the Republic of Belarus. – http://www.belstat.gov.by

26 Based on the data from The National Bank of the Republic of Belarus / http://www.nbrb.by

27 Average for 2016 – 2018.

28 Ibid.

29 Ibid.

30 Bobrovich V. (2014). The FX rate in Belarus within the context of deflationary expectations: abstract, dissertation for candidate of economic sciences. (In Russian) — Minsk: Belarusian State Economic University, 2014. — Pp 23.

31 Rudy K., Uchov A. (2006). Choice of the Exchange Rate Regime: Theory and Practice in the Case of Belarus // International Economics and Finance Journal. — Volume 1. No 2 (December 2006).

32 Reinhart C., Rogoff K. (2012). This Time is Different: Eight Centuries of Financial Folly. — Career Press, 2012. — P. 472.

33 Ibid.

34 Collier P. (2008). The Bottom Billion: Why the Poorest Countries are Failing and What Can Be Done About It. — Oxford University Press, 2008.

35 Vinhas de Souza L. (2014). The CIS and Russia-Ukraine Stresses // Moody's Investors Service. Presentation at Global context, local solutions: Belarus; private sector potential, Minsk. November 5, 2014 — Pp 29.

36 Based on data from the World Bank – http://www.worldbank.org

37 Based on the data from The National Bank of the Republic of Belarus / http://www.nbrb.by

38 Reinert E. (2008). How Rich Countries Got Rich and Why Poor Countries Stay Poor – Constable & Robinson, 2008. — 400 p.

39 Wolf M. (2005). Why Globalization Works / M. Wolf. — Yale: Nota Bene, 2005.
40 Based on the data from The National Bank of the Republic of Belarus / http://www.nbrb.by
41 Gill, I. An East Asian Renaissance: Ideas for Economic Growth / I. Gill, H. Kharas. – Washington: The World Bank, 2007. – 366 p.
42 The World Bank In Middle Income Countries // World Bank. – http://www.worldbank.org/en/country/mic/overview#2.
43 Escaping the Middle Income Trap / Global Economic Symposium. – Режим доступа: http://www.global-economic-symposium.org .
44 Spence, M. The Next Convergence. The Future of Economic Growth in a Multispeed World / M. Spence. – New York: Farrar, Straus and Giroux, 2011. – 320 p.
45 Agenor, P. Avoiding Middle-Income Growth Traps / P. Agenor, O. Canuto, M. Jelenic // World Bank Working Paper. – № 98. – 2012. – 7 p.
46 Rudy K., Bobrovich V., Lashuk I., Urban D. (2018) "Middle-Income Trap": Interdisciplinary Evaluation of the Way Out for Belarus. (In Russian) // Belorusskiy Economicheskiy Journal. – 2018. - №3. – Pp. 4 – 18.
47 Ibid.
48 Based on the data from the National Statistical Committee of the Republic of Belarus. – http://www.belstat.gov.by
49 Based on data from http://www.tradingeconomics.com
50 Shimov V. (2014). Innovative Development of the Belarusian Economy: Drivers and National Priorities: monograph (In Russian) / V. Shimov, L. Kryukov. — Minsk: Belarusian State Economic University, 2014. — Pp 199.
51 Haskel J., Westlake S. (2018) Capitalism without Capital. The Rise of the Intangible Economy. – Princeton University Press. Princeton, 2018. – 278 p.
52 Banerjee A.V., Duflo E. (2019) Good Economics for Hard Times. – Public Affairs, NY. – 2019. – 403 p.
53 Sharygina Y., Sivaev S. (2015). A Comparative Analysis of Utility Available for Citizens of the Russian Federation and Other Countries (In Russian) // Voprosy Economiki. — 2015. — № 6. — Pp. 63–105.
54 Porter M. (2013). Why Business Can Be Good at Solving Social Problems [Electronic resource] // TED Talk, October, 2013. — http://www.ted.com
55 Based on the data from the National Statistical Committee of the Republic of Belarus. – http://www.belstat.gov.by
56 Grove A. (1996). Only the Paranoid Survive: How to Exploit the Crisis Points that Challenge Every Company. — Publishers Weekly, 1996. — Pp 224.
57 Adizes I. (2016). Mastering Change – Introduction to Organization Therapy. – Adizes Institute, 2016. – 298 p.
58 Adizes I. (1999) Managing Corporate Lifecycles. – Prentice Hall, 1999. – 460 p.

59 Gaidar Y. (2006). Collapse of an Empire: Lessons for Modern Russia. (In Russian) — Moscow: Russian Political Encyclopedia, 2006. — Pp 592.
60 Gordon R. (2012). Is US economic growth over? Faltering innovation confronts the six headwinds // CEPR Policy Insight. — No. 63, September 2012.
61 Rogoff K. (2015). Debt supercycle, not secular stagnation [Electronic resource] // CEPR's Policy Portal. — http://www.voxue.org
62 Summers L. (2014). US Economic Prospects: Secular Stagnation, Hysteresis, and the Zero Lower Bound // Business Economics. — Vol. 49. No. 2.
63 Morgan Stanley (2015). The Global Macro Analyst. The Paradox of Secular Stagnation Thesis. — Morgan Stanley Outlook, 2015.
64 Based on the data – http://www.statista.com
65 Piketty T. (2014). Capital in the Twenty-First Century. — Belknap Press, 2014.
66 United Nations (2015). The 2014 Human Development Report Sustaining Human Progress: Reducing Vulnerabilities and Building Resilience [Electronic resource] / http://www.hdr.undp.org.
67 Aven P. (2015). The USSR was a dangerous country, not like Russia today. (In Russian) [Electronic resource] // https://slon.ru
68 Gaidar Y. (2006). Collapse of an Empire: Lessons for Modern Russia. (In Russian) — Moscow: Russian Political Encyclopedia, 2006. — Pp 592.
69 Aslund Anders and Djankov Simeon (2014). The Great Rebirth. Lessons from the Victory of Capitalism over Communism. – Peterson Institute for International Economics, 2014.
70 Based on the data from Transition Report (2003). Integration and regional cooperation. [Electronic resource] / EBRD, 2003.
71 Based on the data from Transition Report (2006). Finance in transition [Electronic resource] / EBRD, 2006.
72 Based on the data from Transition Report (2008). Growth in transition [Electronic resource] / EBRD, 2008.
73 Based on the data from Transition Report (2012). Integration across borders [Electronic resource] / EBRD, 2012.
74 Based on the data from Transition Report (2014). Innovation in transition [Electronic resource] / EBRD, 2014
75 Klein N. (2007). The Shock Doctrine: The Rise of Disaster Capitalism / N. Klein — Metropolitan Books, 2007.
76 IMF (2014) 25 Years of Transition Post-Communist Europe and the IMF / James Roaf, Ruben Atoyan, Bikas Joshi, Krzysztof Krogulski and an IMF Staff Team. — Regional Economic Issues. Special Report, Oct. 2014.
77 Young A. (2002). Economies in Transition: Conception, Status and Prospects / Ed. by A. Young [and others]. — World Scientific Publishing Co. Pte. Ltd., 2002.
78 Sachs J. (1996). Achieving Rapid Growth in the Transition Economies of Central Europe / J. Sachs, A. Warner // Development Discussion Paper № 544.

July 1996. — Cambridge, Mass.: Harvard Institute for International Development, Harvard University.

79 Based on the data from Transition Report (2003). Integration and regional cooperation. [Electronic resource] / EBRD, 2003.

80 Based on the data from Transition Report (2006). Finance in transition [Electronic resource] / EBRD, 2006.

81 Based on the data from Transition Report (2008). Growth in transition [Electronic resource] / EBRD, 2008.

82 Based on the data from Transition Report (2012). Integration across borders [Electronic resource] / EBRD, 2012.

83 Based on the data from Transition Report (2014). Innovation in transition [Electronic resource] / EBRD, 2014

84 Kudrin A., Gurvich E. (2014). A New Growth Model for the Russian Economy (In Russian) // Voprosy Economiki. — 2014. — № 12. — Pp. 4–36.

85 Based on the data from Transition Report (2003). Integrationand regional cooperation. [Electronic resource] / EBRD, 2003.

86 Based on the data from Transition Report (2006). Finance in transition [Electronic resource] / EBRD, 2006.

87 Based on the data from Transition Report (2008). Growth in transition [Electronic resource] / EBRD, 2008.

88 Based on the data from Transition Report (2012). Integration across borders [Electronic resource] / EBRD, 2012.

89 Based on the data from Transition Report (2014). Innovation in transition [Electronic resource] / EBRD, 2014

90 Rudy K., Bobrovich V., Lashuk I., Urban D. (2018) "Middle-Income Trap": Interdisciplinary Evaluation of the Way Out for Belarus. (In Russian) // Belorusskiy Economicheskiy Journal. – 2018. - №3. – Pp. 4 – 18.

91 Berger Y. (2009). Economic Strategy of China (In Russian). – Moscow: "Forum", 2009. – Pp. 559.

92 Wang Y. (2017). Beijing at the Helm. // Forbes Asia. – November, 2017. – Pp. 12 – 13.

93 Walter C.E., Howie F.J.T. Privatizing China. Inside China's Stock Markets. – Singapore: John Wiley & Sons (Asia) Pte Ltd., 2006. – 335 p.

94 Mozias P. (2015). The Chinese Economy: Immersion in a New Normality (In Russian) // Voprosy Economiki. — 2015. — № 5. — Pp. 134–158.

95 Rudy K. (2015). Chinese Lessons // SB — Belarus Today. — 2015. — № 109 dated June 11, 2015.

96 Cao D. (2019). Xi: Step up fight against corruption. // China Daily, January 12 – 13, 2019. – P. 1

97 Zhang Y. (2020). 2019 a big year in anti-corruption fight. // China Daily, January 13, 2020. – Pp. 1, 9.

98 Economy E.C. The Third Revolution. Xi Jinping and the New Chinese State. – Oxford University Press. New York, 2018. – 343 p.

99 Based on the data from The Economist, March 28, 2015.
100 Sinek S. (2011). Start With Why: How Great Leaders Inspire Everyone to Take Action. — Portfolio, 2011. — Pp 256.
101 Collins J. (2001). Good to Great: Why Some Companies Make the Leap…and Others Don't — Harper Business, 2001. — Pp. 400.
102 Adizes I. (1999) Managing Corporate Lifecycles. – Prentice Hall, 1999. – 460 p.
103 Christensen C. (2011). The Innovator's Dilemma: When New Technologies Cause Great Firms to Fail. — Harper Business, 2011. — Pp. 336.
104 Sachs J. (2005). The End of Poverty / J. Sachs. — Penguin Press, 2005.
105 Acemoglu D., Robinson J. (2013). Why Nations Fail: The Origins of Power, Prosperity, and Poverty. — Crown Business, 2013.
106 Porter M. (1998). Comparative Advantage of Nations / M. E. Porter — Second Edition. — New York: Free Press, 1998.
107 Tirole J. (2017). Economics for the Common Good. – Princeton University Press. Princeton, 2017. – 563 p.
108 Grove A. (1996). Only the Paranoid Survive: How to Exploit the Crisis Points that Challenge Every Company. — Publishers Weekly, 1996. — Pp 224.
109 Evstigneeva L., Evstigneev R. (2014) The Contours of a New Economic Space (In Russian) // Voprosy Economiki. — 2014. — № 11. — Pp. 140–155.
110 Grinberg R. (2015). The Pragmatism of the General Economic Theory (regarding Whither the World: The Political Economy of the Future, by Grzegorz Kołodko) (In Russian) // Russian Journal of Economics. — 2015. — № 2. — Pp. 105–115.
111 Kołodko G. (2014). Whither the World: The Political Economy of the Future. (In Russian) — Moscow: Magistr, 2014. — Pp. 528.
112 Yasin, Y. (2015). Positive Economics (In Russian) // Liberal Mission Foundation [Electronic resource]. — http://www.liberal.ru
113 Kapelyushnikov R. (2015). The Idea of a Stagnant Century: Three Versions (In Russian) // Voprosy Economiki. — 2015. — № 5. — Pp. 104–133.
114 Grove A. (1996). Only the Paranoid Survive: How to Exploit the Crisis Points that Challenge Every Company. — Publishers Weekly, 1996. — Pp 224.
115 Tirole J. (2017). Economics for the Common Good. – Princeton University Press. Princeton, 2017. – 563 p.
116 Adizes I. (1999) Managing Corporate Lifecycles. – Prentice Hall, 1999. – 460 p.
117 Chang Ha-Joon. (2008). Bad Samaritans. The Myth of Free Trade and Secret History of Capitalism. – Bloomsbury Press. London, 2008. – 276 p.
118 Grove A. (1996). Only the Paranoid Survive: How to Exploit the Crisis Points that Challenge Every Company. — Publishers Weekly, 1996. — Pp 224.
119 Adizes I. (1999) Managing Corporate Lifecycles. – Prentice Hall, 1999. – 460 p.

120 Reinert E. (2008). How Rich Countries Got Rich and Why Poor Countries Stay Poor – Constable & Robinson, 2008. — 400 p.

121 Christensen C. (2011). The Innovator's Dilemma: When New Technologies Cause Great Firms to Fail. — Harper Business, 2011. — Pp. 336.

122 Collier P. (2018). The Future of Capitalism. Facing the New Anxieties. – Allen Lane. UK, 2018. – 248 p.

123 Lin J. (2012). The Quest for Prosperity. How Developing Economies Can Take Off. — Princeton University Press, 2012.

124 Zuboff Sh. (2019). The Age of Surveillance Capitalism. – New York: Public Affairs, 2019. – 691 p.

125 Rudy K. (2001). Features of Currency Boards in Foreign Countries (In Russian) // Association of Belarusian Banks Newsletter. — 2001. — № 39. — Pp. 37–46.

126 Saxena N.C. (2011). Virtuous Cycles: The Singapore Public Service and National Development. – UNDP, 2011. – 200 p.

127 Snyder T. (2018). The Road to Unfreedom. Russia, Europe, America. – Vintage. London, 2018. – 359 p.